English Language Learners and the New Standards

English Language Learners and the New Standards

◆

Developing Language, Content Knowledge, and
Analytical Practices in the Classroom

Margaret Heritage
Aída Walqui
Robert Linquanti

Harvard Education Press
Cambridge, Massachusetts

Third Printing, 2016

Library of Congress Control Number 2014959081

Paperback ISBN 978-1-61250-801-6
Library Edition ISBN 978-1-61250-802-3

Published by Harvard Education Press,
an imprint of the Harvard Education Publishing Group

Harvard Education Press
8 Story Street
Cambridge, MA 02138

Cover Design: Joel Gendron
Cover Photo: Blend Images – Hill Street Studios/Brand X Pictures/Getty Images
The typefaces used in this book are Minion Pro and Myriad Pro

In memory of Leo van Lier, a remarkable scholar, teacher, and human being.

Contents

◆

Foreword

———————◆———————

We educators are in Wave 3 of standards-based reform—the third successive wave of energy unleashed by *A Nation at Risk*.

The first wave started over thirty years ago, in the throes of the Reagan administration, when many of us were still tinkering with the early toys of the computer revolution and Ford Pintos were exploding upon impact, signaling the decline of American industry. Concerned, the nation marched into the world of standards-based education to improve our schools. *A Nation at Risk* was published in 1983 and launched a string of federally encouraged state-led efforts to improve education through aspiration for world-class standards. Governor Bill Clinton joined the act and passed signature legislation when he became President, known as Improving America's Schools Act, setting state standards in place.

Wave 2 came as No Child Left Behind, under George W. Bush, adding teeth to the assessment system for purposes of accountability. During this wave, the section of the law that provides federal aid to English language learners (ELLs), known as Title III, added assessment of student English language proficiency (ELP) as a requirement, and an accountability system was set up to set performance targets, monitor results, and require corrective actions.

And now we have a commitment to a new set of standards for "college and career readiness," which in many states are referred to as the Common Core State Standards and the Next Generation Science Standards. Starting in 2015, new assessment systems will be in place in many states to measure student proficiency in these standards. Also available will be new assessment systems for the English language proficiency of ELLs that are aligned to revised ELP standards that "correspond" to the language demands inherent in the content standards. These new and demanding standards represent the third wave of standards-based reform.

The authors of this book describe education policy as "a prescribed course of action that encodes key values of those that make and enact policy prescriptions." In all three waves of reform, the "encoded key value" in the policy has been an emphasis on assessment for accountability purposes. This emphasis is due to the governing philosophy of "deregulation and flexibility in exchange for results"—a system that provides incentives and penalties for outcomes (rather than focusing on regulating inputs), and lets the invisible hand guide the actions of systems. This idea started with Reagan, was embraced by Clinton, and grew teeth under G. W. Bush.

In *English Language Learners and the New Standards*, Margaret Heritage, Aída Walqui, and Robert Linquanti perform a remarkable *jujitsu* act—taking the energy of this wave of reform and training it on the context of instruction. What this book tells us, and illustrates through a portrayal of learning processes and learning progressions in real classrooms, is that this emphasis on assessment for accountability generates a systemic focus on results, but does not travel further to instruction. The authors' *jujitsu* act is to build a channel that guides this energy by emphasizing the kinds of instructional practices that exemplify learning and support individual student learning. That is to say, formative assessment is highlighted, featured, and modeled as a set of practices that supports student learning, rather than as an external agent of system, teacher, and student accountability.

The ambitious and sophisticated nature of this work is reflected by the range of knowledge, expertise, and experience of the three authors. Margaret Heritage is best known as the articulate and passionate spokesperson for the understanding of formative assessment practice. She has spent much of her career illustrating and advocating for what Black and Wiliam characterize as a "process used by teachers to recognize and respond to student learning, in order to enhance that learning, during the learning." Aída Walqui is a highly accomplished champion of teacher professional development who has moved the field of English language learners from a bifurcated view of learning (in this class, we work on the student's grammar, and in that class, we work on math) to an integrated one. Throughout her career, by her actions as well as by her shaping of the theoretical literature on second-language acquisition, she has created pathways between the two solitudes—the ESL teacher and the "mainstream" content teacher. And Robert Linquanti is the prime "policy wonk" of systems of assessment and accountability for ELLs, and has analyzed and surfed the successive waves of reform with an eye to giving all students access to meeting the standards. He is probably the most influential policy analyst and actor in the field for states and many school districts.

The book has an ambitious agenda, bringing these formidable actors together to provide a narrative to model and envision what assessment practice must look like during the present context of reform. It creates pathways between assessment and instruction, policy and practice, and above all, between language and academic content. Undoubtedly, the will for reform is still generated by the philosophy of flexibility of means for accountability of results. However, this book takes this framework and illustrates *how* the teaching profession can adapt and shape instruction for ELLs based on continual evidence of student learning. This is a deft move, and could not have been made at a better moment.

As the nation moves to the implementation of the new standards, readers will find great inspiration in the authors' vision of what learning can become for ELLs, and in their real examples of the powerful pedagogy, responsive assessment, and coherent policy required to get there.

—Kenji Hakuta
Lee L. Jacks Professor of Education
Stanford Graduate School of Education

CHAPTER 1

ELLs and the New Standards

Meeting the Goals of College and Career Readiness

Students who are English language learners (ELLs) represent close to 10 percent of the total student population in the United States and make up its most rapidly growing sector.[1] The number of students who are ELLs has grown from two million to five million since 1990, vastly outpacing the growth in the overall school population.[2] However, in general, academic outcomes for ELLs remain stubbornly low. For example, according to data on reading performance from the National Assessment of Educational Progress (NAEP), in 2013, on a 0–500 scale, the achievement gap between non-ELL and ELL students was 38 points at the fourth-grade level and 45 points at the eighth-grade level. At both grade levels, the 2013 reading achievement gap was not measurably different from the gap in either 2011 or 1998, when NAEP first started collecting data on ELL students' status.[3] Equally worrying is the situation in mathematics: in 2013, on a scale of 0–500, the achievement gap between non-ELL and ELL students was 25 points at the fourth-grade level and 41 points at the eighth-grade level.[4] At both grades, this achievement gap was broadly similar to the gap in 1996.[5]

Against this background of ELL performance, the most recent reform effort in American education is the introduction of college and career ready standards, which are intended to ensure that when students graduate from high school they will be equipped with the necessary knowledge and skills essential for future success.[6] College and career ready standards are a response to ongoing globalization and represent current societal expectations of the competencies U.S. students need to acquire to be productive citizens and effective contributors to a vibrant economy. No doubt the current college and career ready standards will undergo revisions and perhaps a major overhaul in the long term as the world continues to change and requirements for students need to adapt accordingly. Nonetheless, the current college and career ready standards represent some significant transformations about what students need to learn and how teachers need to teach, and they are likely to be in place for a considerable time to come. Examples of college and career ready standards include the Common Core State Standards (CCSS) for English language arts (ELA) and mathematics, the Next Generation Science Standards (NGSS), and corresponding standards and frameworks for English language development.[7]

An examination of college and career ready standards reveals their emphasis on extensive language use to engage in deep and transferable content learning and analytical practices. For example, in terms of analytical practices, the NGSS require students to ask questions, construct explanations, argue from evidence, and obtain, evaluate, and communicate information.[8] The mathematics CCSS ask students to explain, conjecture, and justify in making sense of problems and solving them, and to construct viable arguments and critique the reasoning of others.[9] And among the ELA analytical practices are: engaging with complex texts; writing to inform, argue, and analyze; working collaboratively; and presenting ideas.[10]

The introduction of college and career ready standards by most states in the United States presents both a challenge and an opportunity for ELLs, who regularly must do "double the work"—acquire content knowledge and analytical practices at the same time as they are learning English as an additional language.[11] The challenge lies in the heightened demands of the standards in terms of content expectations and what students are required to do with language as they engage in content-area learning.[12] If ELL students have not been successful with prior standards, then it is highly likely that achieving more demanding ones will be challenging.

However, if the introduction of college and career ready standards represents a challenge for ELLs, it also presents an opportunity. College and career ready standards imply significant changes in educational practice, in which ELLs learn language and content simultaneously. This reformulation involves practice that is consistent with the view among second-language experts that when teachers construct powerful invitations to engage ELL students in language use in worthwhile disciplinary contexts, they can develop conceptual understandings, analytical practices, and dynamic language use in the domain, enabling them to succeed in school and beyond.[13] An added advantage is that effective pedagogy for ELLs will be equally beneficial for native speakers of English who are not doing well academically because they speak a nonstandard variety of English, and have not been appropriately assisted to learn the academic and more formal uses of the language. This book is about the reformulation of practice to achieve these outcomes.

In this reformulation of practice, preparing ELL students to achieve the language and learning expectations of college and career ready standards is not the sole responsibility of a small cadre of language specialists teaching English-as-a-second-language (ESL) classes. For children entering school with little or no English, there is a pivotal role for ESL teachers to develop students' initial English language, both social and academic, in deep, accelerated ways. However, once students have moved beyond the emergent level of proficiency in English, further development of the academic uses of language becomes the responsibility of every teacher.[14] Also, teachers in math, ELA, and science cannot do all the heavy lifting. They need the support of their colleagues in other disciplines to engage ELLs in meaningful language use for discipline-specific purposes. For example, in art, students might be asked to justify their use of particular color or line forms; in physical education, students may have to explain or negotiate the rules of a game; and similarly in history/social studies, students could be asked to discuss evidence for certain claims they are making about the causes of the Civil War.[15] And when teachers in other disciplines attend to ELL students' language development, they will surely benefit the learning of their own subjects.

Assessment is an integral component of the reformulation of practice we propose. In this regard, we do not mean assessment through quizzes or other testlike events, but rather assessment that involves teachers in gathering evidence of both language and content learning *while* that learning is taking place, so that they can use the evidence to engage in contingent pedagogy. When pedagogy is contingent upon the students' current learning status, the teacher is essentially meeting the student where he or she is at that moment in learning. In other words, the teacher is matching her pedagogy to the student's immediate needs in order to move learning forward. When a teacher's pedagogy is contingent, she is consistently working in and through each student's zone of proximal development—the bandwidth of competence that currently exists and that, with assistance, learners can navigate to a more advanced state of understanding or skill.[16]

Assessment to support contingent pedagogy also enables student involvement in the assessment process, through peer and self-assessment. Providing opportunities for student involvement in assessment encourages student agency in learning, helping them develop desirable college and career ready skills such as responsibility, self-direction, self-monitoring, collaboration, and cooperation.

This book is about how *all* teachers can assist ELL students to successfully meet the rigorous demands of college and career ready standards by engaging them in the simultaneous learning of content, analytical practices, and language learning, supported by ongoing assessment and contingent pedagogy.

So far, we have referred to the population of students in U.S. schools who are learning English as an additional language with the single term ELL. In fact, ELL students are a very diverse group.[17] In the section below, we consider the range of backgrounds that ELLs represent in our schools.

Who are ELLs?

Among the variables accounting for the diversity of ELLs in the United States are:

- **Time in the United States.** In some classrooms, students may be newly arrived in the United States, others may have spent more time in the United States, and still others will have been born and raised in the United States.

- **Experience of formal schooling.** Students who are new to the United States, even if they are beyond kindergarten age, may have variations in their experience of formal schooling in their country of prior residence; so too with migrant students living in the United States.
- **Language status.** Students may be monolingual, speaking only a language other than English; bilingual, speaking two languages other than English; emergent bilinguals, developing English as they continue to expand their competence in their already established first language; or they may be multilingual, speaking several languages other than English.
- **Exposure to English.** Because of their varying background circumstances, time in the United States, and time in school, students will have different levels of exposure to English.
- **Ethnic heritage.** Students may be members of different ethnic groups and, as such, represent differences in ancestry, culture, and, of course, language.
- **Developmental differences.** It is axiomatic that ELLs will not develop in their language or content learning at the same rate or the same pace or in the same way.

What this list tells us is that no two ELLs are the same. They bring to the classroom diverse experiences, interests, and languages. It follows then that a one-size-fits-all approach to supporting ELLs' learning will not meet the needs of all students. While the goals for ELLs are equivalent to those for their English-proficient peers—reaching high standards set forth in the new standards—their pathways to attaining the standards may not be. ELL teachers are sensitive and responsive to who their students are, to the resources they bring to the classroom, and to how their students' learning of content, analytical practices, and language is developing day-by-day in the classroom. Only this kind of sensitivity and responsiveness brings about the successful accomplishment of learning for ELLs in the nation's classrooms.

Let us now turn to an example of a classroom where the teacher's practice corresponds to the reformulation of pedagogy in which learning content, analytical practices, and language occur simultaneously. In this classroom, which includes a range of ELL students, assessment is integrated into ongoing teaching and learning.[18]

◆

Learning Science Content, Analytical Practices, and Language Together

The third-grade students, all from economically poor backgrounds, are mostly designated ELL and have varying levels of English language proficiency. Some students have very little English yet; others' English is more developed; and still others are well on their way to becoming very competent English users. Some students are new to the United States, while others have been born to recent immigrant families. All the students who entered kindergarten at the school began as non-English speakers. Since kindergarten, the approach of all their teachers has been to develop content learning, analytical practices, and language simultaneously. As you will see, the rate of language growth for many students has been very fast.

Throughout this vignette, notice how language learning is not regarded as an individual endeavor, and how the students receive many invitations to engage with each other and their teacher to use and develop their English language skills through purposeful communicative activities in content-area learning. In a real sense the students are apprentices in learning language and content together. Apprenticeship involves learning target skills in a social context, a community of learners in this case. Apprentices also learn through modeling, with appropriate support when needed, and coaching, which we will see in the vignette.[19]

Notice, too, the participant structures that the teacher has established. Students are provided with many opportunities to engage in discourse and have been taught how to participate in the discourse practices of the classroom, listening carefully to their peers, building on each other's ideas, and giving constructive feedback. The classroom is characterized by notions of joint responsibility for the learning of all students as well as the responsibility individuals have for their own learning.[20] In this classroom, students are supported to adopt the stance of generativity and autonomy. In other words, students are developing the skills to support their own learning by using independently what they have learned in the context of engaging with peers and the teacher within a well-structured classroom community.[21]

Notice also how the teacher supports her students' language learning through specific pedagogical approaches. She very deliberately models the language she wishes her students to acquire; she provides formulaic expressions—chunks of language the ELLs learn as a unit that enable them to participate in interactions; and she offers prompts and feedback to support language and content learning.[22]

And finally, pay attention to how the teacher engages in ongoing assessment of her students and helps them to undertake both peer and self-assessment.

Research Study on Desert Cactuses

The purpose of the students' research study is to support the class's science focus for the quarter and to contribute to the students' developing understanding that organisms "have both internal and external structures that allow for growth, survival, behavior and reproduction."[23] In addition to the science focus, their teacher, Ms. Cardenas, has identified several Common Core ELA standards that she wishes to address in this research project.[24] These include:

Key Ideas and Details

CCSS.ELA-Literacy.RI.3.1: Ask and answer questions to demonstrate understanding of a text, referring explicitly to the text as the basis for the answers.

Craft and Structure

CCSS.ELA-Literacy.RI.3.5: Use text features and search tools (e.g., key words, sidebars, hyperlinks) to locate information relevant to a given topic efficiently.

Writing

CCSS.ELA-Literacy.W.3.7: Conduct short research projects that build knowledge about a topic.

CCSS.ELA-Literacy.W.3.8: Recall information from experiences or gather information from print and digital sources; take brief notes on sources and sort evidence into provided categories.

Speaking and Listening

CCSS.ELA-Literacy.SL.3.4: Report on a topic or text, tell a story, or recount an experience with appropriate facts and relevant, descriptive details, speaking clearly at an understandable pace.

Preparation

To begin the study, Ms. Cardenas takes her students on a field trip to a desert garden. The students make detailed observational drawings of cactuses in their sketchbooks. While they are drawing, Ms. Cardenas focuses their observation through questioning:

What do you notice?

What are some similarities and differences between the plants you see here and the plants we have at school?

Why do you think the plants have these particular features?

Through these questions, she is modeling the language that she would like students to use in the discussions they will have about cactuses.

After they have drawn several cactuses, the students gather together and in pairs share their observations and their theories about why the cactuses have the features they do. In this activity, they are engaged in analytical practices. The students use formulaic expressions they have learned in class in other contexts, such as "I noticed that . . . ," "my prediction is that they have these features because . . . ," and "what makes you say that?" Ms. Cardenas listens in on the conversations so that she can hear the kinds of questions they are asking each other, note the language they are using, and determine their level of background knowledge related to the function of the desert plants' external structures. She will use this information to assist students in developing their ideas and language during their study.

Developing questions

Back in the classroom with their drawings, the students respond to Ms. Cardenas's question, Based on your observations, what would you like to know or are unsure of about desert plants? Each child writes his or her question on a large sentence strip, and then all the students share their questions, in turn, with their classmates. As a whole class, they then discuss all twenty-eight of the questions they created and begin categorizing them according to the focus of the question, or, as one student said, "by what the question is asking." During this process, the students agree and disagree about where different questions belong. Below is an excerpt from the students' discussion as they consider the questions:

> "Why some cactuses have hair on them?" and "Why cactus has [*sic*] sticks and not leaf?"—They want to know about how cactus is on the outside.
>
> Even though "Why can cactuses survive with less water than plants here at school?" is a question about cactus, it is different from the first two questions because it is asking not so much about how a cactus looks, but about what it needs to survive.
>
> I disagree because the hairs on a cactus and the reason they don't have leaves might be because that [*sic*] they don't get enough water.
>
> I see what you are saying, but since we don't know that for sure, I think it goes in a different category.

Notice the variations in English proficiency represented in these examples. There are some grammatical errors, which Ms. Cardenas does not correct on the spot. She wants her students to feel confident in using English at whatever level they have acquired, realizing that in order to learn English her students need to use it. She pays attention to the grammatical errors (e.g., "Why cactus has [*sic*] sticks and not leaf"), and in subsequent interactions with this student—and other students who make the same errors—she models the correct use of the grammatical structure ("Why do cactuses have . . .?") and prompts students to incorporate this language in her interactions with them.

Categorizing questions

At this point, Ms. Cardenas introduces three category questions: inch, foot, and yard, shown in the classroom chart (figure 1.1), and engages the

FIGURE 1.1   Question category chart

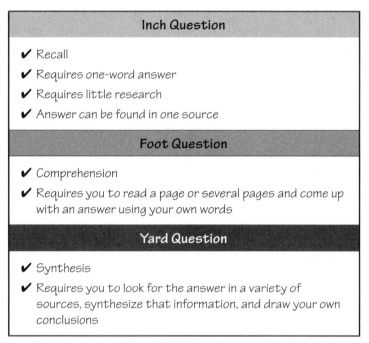

students in a discussion about what makes them different from each other. As a whole class they discuss the question categories (inch, foot, yard) and decide that their first research question will be a yard question, Why do cactuses have spines?

The students revisit their initial sketches, and, engaging in analytical practice, they write predictions about why they think cactuses have spines. Figure 1.2 shows an example of one student's prediction on a sticky note, which he places on his drawing in his sketchbook.

After they have written their individual predictions, they meet in pairs to share and discuss each person's response. These paired discussions give Ms. Cardenas the chance to listen to their language and ascertain what evidence they used to support their thinking about the prediction. After participating in the discussion, some students revise their ideas and note their revisions on a sticky note in their sketchbooks. Figure 1.3 shows one student's revised thinking.

FIGURE 1.2   Student's prediction

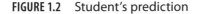

I think the spines are like
weapons for the cactus
because they are sharp

Research and synthesis

To begin their research, the students read a variety of text passages about desert plants that Ms. Cardenas has carefully chosen from a range of sources. In prior lessons, students have learned about the structure of informational text and how to use certain features such as headings, subheadings, and illustrations. They have also learned how to identify key details in a text. Ms. Cardenas has modeled how to highlight key information related to a specific question and to make notes from the highlighted text, and she has conducted think-alouds about what to do with "tricky" words or a "tricky" part of the text.

FIGURE 1.3   Student revision

OH I thought they were like
bones because thea re hard
but now I think they are
trapers.

Ms. Cardenas has taught her students to read "with the question in mind," and to support this process, she has provided them with a set of questions:

Does this fact from the text help answer my question?

What about this fact helps answer my question?

How do I know?

What words and sentences in the text help me think that?

During the time that children are reading, highlighting their text, and making notes, Ms. Cardenas has brief individual conferences with each student. The purpose of the conferences is to assess how well the students are capturing relevant information through their highlighting and note taking, and to take account of the words and phrases they are finding new or challenging. At the end of each conference, she provides the student with feedback that helps him or her improve his or her reading and information-gathering strategies. Here is an example of the feedback Ms. Cardenas gives to one student:

I see you have gathered plenty of valuable information about desert cactuses. I'm wondering if all this information is necessary to help answer the question, Why do cactuses have spines? What do you think?

And to another student:

Can I suggest that as you continue to gather information, you take a moment to revisit the question and ask yourself, does this help answer the question? If it doesn't, maybe you can organize your notes by highlighting these facts in a different color, so you know where to find other information about cactuses. Maybe this will help organize your information and keep you focused on the research question. What do you think?

As they collect the information relevant to their question, the students regularly discuss their findings with a partner, compare notes, and provide each other with feedback. As we have seen, feedback is something the teacher models as a routine practice with students. Below is some of the feedback excerpted from the students' conversations during their peer-assessment sessions:

> **Nico:** I like how you are using key words when taking notes and not copying from your reading.
>
> **Eva:** Are the notes you take from the highlighted sections of your reading passage?
>
> **Diego:** You can highlight everywhere information so you know where it is from. This help you organize.

Notice in this feedback the precise language that students use. Ms. Cardenas is very deliberate in her language choices, and the students have been exposed to this language when Ms. Cardenas models reading and note taking. Now the students are incorporating the language they have heard into their own usage.

Once the students think they have sufficient information, they begin the process of synthesizing it. Individually, they sort through their notes, reviewing their information with the same questions that guided their note taking. Then, in pairs, they combine their information, and on large poster paper, they jot down their findings. As they do this, Ms. Cardenas circulates among the pairs to see how well they are synthesizing and combining their notes. Here is another opportunity for her to provide feedback to help the students improve their work.

Product and presentation

When the students have completed all their research, the final phase of the study begins. In small groups, the children make large cactus sculptures that represent what they have learned as a result of their research. Using an organizer Ms. Cardenas has provided, the students begin their work together by translating their notes into a blueprint for their sculpture, deciding what key features of the cactus they wish to represent. Developing the blueprint involves a great deal of discussion among the students. Next, from their blueprint and using a wide range of materials—found objects and recyclables that Ms. Cardenas has provided—they work together over the course of several days to create their sculpture.

It is noteworthy that Ms. Cardenas very carefully selects the composition of all the groups in the classroom, from partner work for peer assessment and feedback to the small groups creating their sculptures. She wants to make sure that there is a range of English language proficiency represented in the groups so that students whose English language is not as developed as others' have a chance to hear more proficient models.

When creating their sculptures, the students use language for a variety of purposes: referring back to the information on their blueprint, justifying why they want the sculpture to develop in certain ways, negotiating the materials they use, and making suggestions about how to improve their sculpture. Ms. Cardenas uses these discussions as opportunities to listen in and scaffold students' language use.[25] For example, "I see you have labeled the spines on your sculpture. I wonder why this cactus has these spines—what is their function? Can you help me understand the function in your sculpture?" and "You have used very descriptive words to help me understand the texture of the cactus—thick and waxy—why would a cactus have a thick, waxy skin? Can you help me understand that better?" When the sculptures are developed to the students' satisfaction, some of the groups decide to put explanatory written labels on certain features of their cactuses in response to Ms. Cardenas's feedback and their peers' assessment. Below are examples of two different groups' labels:

Group 1: Areole
An important part of protecting the cactus.
Big leaves to absorb water would and lose to [*sic*] much water.

Areole
Are almost round but always hold the spines.

Group 2: Thick waxy coating
The thick waxy coating holds all the water.

Stem
The stem holds water for hot days ahead

Spine
The spines protect the Teddy Bear Cactus from other animals snacking on it and they also give it shade.

The culminating part of the research project is students' oral presentations about the sculptures. To assist the students in structuring their oral presentations, Ms. Cardenas provides an outline and reviews what is expected of both the presenters and the audience. The students work in their small groups on their presentations. During this time, Ms. Cardenas moves from group to group, noting their sentence structures, vocabulary use, and the clarity of their explanations. She uses the information she gains from these observations to provide on-the-spot feedback to students. For example, she asked one group to think about the clarity of their explanations and to pay attention specifically to connecting their ideas. She also uses the information to decide on any subsequent minilessons she wants to conduct with the whole class to strengthen students' language use; for instance, a follow-up on the use of causal connectors (e.g., *because, consequently, for this reason*) to strengthen the connectedness of their discourse.

The students spend three class periods on their presentations, and when the day of the presentations arrives, the groups take turns in showing their sculpture and talking about their findings. As each group finishes, the rest of the students have an opportunity to ask clarifying questions, which prompt the presenters to explain their ideas further, and to provide feedback about what the presenters did well and what they could do to improve. The students' feedback is guided by the expectations they discussed at the outset of the presentation work. Similarly, because Ms. Cardenas also provided the students with clear expectations about the role of the audience, the presenters provide feedback to the audience as well. Some of the presenters' feedback includes: "I liked how your clarifying question made me think more about the function; the audience respect our ideas; I noticed that Sophia was listening with her mind and her heart" (listening with both mind and heart is the term Ms. Cardenas uses to help the students understand the importance of listening to understand and listening with respect).

After all groups have presented their work, students reflect on and revise any of their prior work. One student heard the word *foragers* in one of the presentations and made a connection to a previous observation he had recorded in his sketchbook about the cactus. He found the relevant sticky note in his sketchbook, put a line through his original selection, *animals*, and replaced it with the more precise word *foragers* (see figure 1.4).

FIGURE 1.4   Student revision

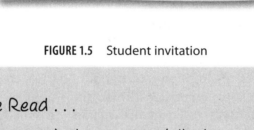

FIGURE 1.5   Student invitation

The morning after the presentations, the students set up their classroom like a gallery and invite visitors from other classes to view their exhibition, learn about desert cactuses, and provide feedback. Some groups write invitations to give feedback and leave them next to the sculptures. One of the student invitations is pictured in figure 1.5. All the students in Ms. Cardenas's class are very proud of their work.

Supporting ELLs' Development of Content, Analytical Practices, and Language

As we noted earlier, Ms. Cardenas's classroom exemplifies effective pedagogy that supports language learning situated in content-area learning. Importantly, while there is variation in the levels of English proficiency in her class, no matter what level of English the students have attained, Ms. Cardenas does not prioritize low-level language skills over opportunities for the students to actively communicate about their ideas. Nor does Ms. Cardenas drill her students in structures and vocabulary in isolation, centered on ensuring correctness and fluency in their language use. Instead, her students are involved in language learning that is focused on comprehension and communication in the context of worthwhile activity designed to advance their learning toward meeting both ELA and science standards.

It is evident in the vignette that Ms. Cardenas has also created routines, norms, and structures in her classroom that permit students to be participants in a community of practice.[26] The expectation that everyone can and will participate in learning together is clearly established. Through the range of participant structures Ms. Cardenas provides— from pairs to small groups to the whole class—her students are invited to contribute to each other's learning. Students know that whatever level of English they have acquired will not be ridiculed by their teacher or peers. They also know that when they express their ideas and understanding, there will be no negative responses but only constructive feedback. Every day Ms. Cardenas models careful attentive listening to what her students say and shows respect for the ideas they share and for their levels of English proficiency. The attitudes, values, and behaviors that Ms. Cardenas models exert a powerful influence on the students' interactions and relationships with each other.[27]

The community of practice that Ms. Cardenas and her students have fashioned together is participant oriented, with structures and expectations in place that permit ELL students, in particular, to develop the identities of confident, committed, and capable language learners.[28] A community of practice is needed for the pedagogical and assessment practices we propose, and we shall return to it in subsequent chapters.

ASSESSMENT

During the course of the students' research study, Ms. Cardenas continuously gathers information about students' learning through her observations and interactions with students and from examining their work products. This process enables her pedagogical responses, including her feedback, to be contingent upon students' current level of content and language learning. Of course, the school uses the results of other assessments, including periodic benchmarks and annual assessments of English language proficiency and of college and career ready standards for a range of decision-making purposes, from curricular modifications to professional learning opportunities, but what matters most to Ms. Cardenas in her daily instructional practice is the emphasis in her school on assessment integrated into ongoing teaching and learning.

Ms. Cardenas also involves students in the assessment process, structuring opportunities for self-assessment, for example, by providing review questions as students collect information related to their investigations. In addition, students are invited to engage in peer assessment, providing feedback to each other that helps them reflect on their work. Recall the various opportunities structured into the work sessions, such as when the students provided feedback to each other on the notes they had taken from their reading, or after the presentations of their findings with the sculptures. As we saw, Ms. Cardenas models feedback to the students through her own feedback to them. The students' ability to provide feedback has been developed through her minilessons on how to give feedback and through her offering students formulaic language expressions (e.g., *could you explain, I respectfully disagree, have you thought about*) that the students incorporate to ensure that the feedback is constructive. She recognizes that developing students' skills in giving and receiving feedback is an ongoing process, and she constantly monitors the students' feedback, offering guidance to individuals and small groups when necessary.

Ms. Cardenas has developed her skills in pedagogy and formative assessment through continuous professional learning opportunities with her colleagues and regular feedback from the principal about her actual classroom practice. Her own experience has accustomed her to professional evaluation—including actionable peer and administrator feedback—that is formative in nature. Moreover, she is used to engaging with her peers in pedagogical planning, including implementing assessment to guide teaching and learning. These support structures and processes have been built into the professional fabric of the school by a committed administrator who understands the value of joint planning for language and content learning with integrated assessment, and who is encouraged and supported to do so by district instructional leaders. This support stands in contrast to many teachers' experiences, as we will discuss in chapter 6. Ms. Cardenas considers herself very fortunate to work and learn in a school and district that have this orientation, and to have access to the professional learning opportunities that are available to her.

Overview of the Chapters

In the chapters that follow, we address in detail the changes in pedagogy that ELL teachers need to make to achieve the aspirations of college and career ready standards with their students. These practices are brought to life through vignettes of real teachers' actual classroom practice so that we can see what the practices entail and what knowledge and skills teachers need to accomplish them. We also consider the theoretical perspectives that have historically influenced teachers' approach to ELL students, and present newer conceptions of teaching and learning for ELLs, grounded in contemporary theory that underpins the practices we describe. Because assessment in its many forms informs pedagogy and many other decisions related to ELLs, we devote two chapters to assessment. In the final chapter, we evaluate the impact and potential of policy on ELLs' learning

Chapter 2

In this chapter we focus on the reformulation of practice that embraces the simultaneous development of ELLs' content knowledge and language proficiency. The chapter begins with a discussion of the language-related shifts in instruction that stem from the standards and from recent developments in theory. These shifts are illustrated through detailed examples of classroom practice, showing how the task of successfully educating

ELLs for deeper learning in an era of college and career ready standards can be accomplished.

Chapter 3

Most teachers think of themselves as practitioners rather than theoreticians, but nearly all teachers' practice is guided by theory, whether consciously or not. This chapter discusses theories that have traditionally shaped teachers' pedagogical practices for ELLs, and describes their benefits and limitations. The chapter brings us up to date about recent developments in second-language acquisition that challenge deep-seated assumptions of language teaching, and that ground the idea of reformulated practice to support ELLs in meeting college and career ready standards described in the previous chapter.

Chapter 4

Continuing the theme of the reformulation of practices, this chapter addresses assessment integrated into instruction—formative assessment. Through examples of practice, we show how teachers can collect evidence of language and content learning through classroom talk and other means, engage in contingent pedagogy based on the evidence obtained, and involve students in assessment through self- and peer assessment, all in the service of simultaneously learning content, analytical practices, and language.

Chapter 5

Beyond immediate teaching and learning in the classroom, educators use assessments to make a range of decisions about ELLs. Beginning with a discussion of how students enter and exit the status of ELL, this chapter focuses on assessments that have a significant impact on ELLs and elaborates on the caution that educators need to take when using the assessments. The chapter also presents some innovations in assessment for ELLs that have the potential to mitigate some of the problems discussed in the chapter with respect to assessing ELL students.

Chapter 6

The final chapter considers the role that policy plays in the education of ELLs. It suggests ways in which educators can both respond to and influence policy to meet the goals of the college and career ready standards for ELLs. The chapter also describes how educators can inform policies that support a learning culture for ELLs and their teachers.

We end this introductory chapter with a quote from Alexei Leontiev, a Russian psychologist who worked with Vygotsky. This quote represents a motif for the book—one that we hope will provide inspiration and guidance for our readers: our goal is to help the child "become what he is not yet."[29]

CHAPTER 2

◆

Changing Times, Changing Teacher Expertise

*Pedagogical Shifts That Support
Ambitious Learning for ELLs*

C ollege and career ready standards have ushered in an era of reform in U.S. education. In chapter 1, we noted that the college and career ready standards place increased demands on all students, and in particular on ELLs. We also discussed that ensuring that ELLs meet the standards requires a reformulation in teachers' classroom practices. In this chapter, we focus on this reformulation of pedagogy for ELL students, which involves a series of shifts in the design of learning materials and pedagogical approaches.[1]

Understanding and implementing these pedagogical shifts is pivotal to success in the education of future generations of ELLs. We characterize the shifts in table 2.1 below.[2] The "From" column represents much of contemporary pedagogical practices with ELLs, while the "To" column signals the shifts that we propose that ELL teachers need to make in their pedagogy.

TABLE 2.1   Shifts in Pedagogy for ELLs

From. . .	To. . .
seeing language acquisition as an individual process	understanding it as a social process of apprenticeship
conceptualizing language in terms of structures or functions	understanding language as action
seeing language acquisition as a linear and progressive process aimed at accuracy, fluency, and complexity	understanding that acquisition occurs in non-linear and complex ways
emphasizing discrete structural features of language	showing how language is purposeful and patterned
lessons focused on individual ideas or texts	cluster of lessons centered on texts that are interconnected by purpose or by theme
activities that pre-teach content	activities that scaffold students' development and autonomy as learners
establishing separate objectives for language and content learning	establishing objectives that integrate language and content learning
using simple or simplified texts	using complex, amplified texts
teaching traditional grammar	teaching multimodal grammar
the use of tests designed by others	the use of formative assessment

◆

Changing the Nature of Teacher Expertise

L et us begin our exploration of the shifts with a vignette that illustrates some of the major changes required to build college and career readiness for ELLs.

Tanya Warren, a teacher at the International Newcomer Academy in Fort Worth, Texas, a high school that receives newly arrived immigrant teenagers for one year before they are transferred to their community schools, is teaching her science class. Her students come from diverse language, cultural, political, and educational backgrounds. It is mid-October, and her students have been working in English for five and a half weeks. In Ms. Warren's class, there are a few students who have had uninterrupted schooling in their home countries; the large majority, however, have experienced major interruptions in their lives and schooling.

While Ms. Warren hands out materials for the main lesson activity on subatomic particles, a slide is projected onto the whiteboard with directions for the first task of the day. "Before we start our investigation," Ms. Warren announces, "we need to think about what we already know." Directing students' attention to the handout, she points to the front page, which contains pictures of items students are familiar with, each object named by a label beginning with the prefix "sub" (such as "submarine"). Students are directed to look at the pictures with a partner, to take turns reading the labels, and to then discuss the guiding question, What do you think the word "sub" means?

At one table, María and José work together. María uses the question written on her paper and says, "What do you think the word 'sub' means?" She pauses. "I think sub means below or under. What do you think, José?" He nods. "Yeah, under. SUBmarine." He makes a gesture with his hand, miming a submarine diving under the water.

After they decide on their answers, Ms. Warren asks students at the different tables to share their answers, and she records them on the board. "Now that you have an idea of what 'sub' means," she tells them, moving them into the next part of the activity, "I want you to write what you think the word 'subatomic' might mean. I also think it might help if you draw a picture of what you think subatomic might mean on your whiteboard." At their tables, groups of four students using their definitions of "sub" work to come up with a collective answer and to draw an accompanying picture. After a few minutes, Ms. Warren invites students to take their pictures to the front of the room so that groups can share them with the class.

Juan, sharing his team's picture, says, "We think the word subatomic means the structure inside the atom." Representing the next team, María traces the picture she and her partners have drawn of a large circle with a smaller core inside as she says, "The subatomic is under, under the atoms." She makes a gesture with her hand moving downward to emphasize "under." "OK, under," confirms Ms. Warren. "Great job!"

With the pictures on the whiteboards lined up behind her, Ms. Warren gestures to the drawings. "You all did a great job of using the idea of 'sub' as down, or under. And here there's even this word, 'inside.' And here you drew inside of the atom. And if we keep going down and down and down, and smaller and smaller and smaller"—here Ms. Warren punctuates her words by making circles with her hands, which become smaller and smaller as she moves downward toward the floor—"what do we have?"

"Subatomic," several students respond in chorus.

"Smaller, inside. Yes, so subatomic means inside, smaller than atoms." She moves to the next slide on her whiteboard, displaying the next set of written directions. "Now we are going to watch a simulation. First you are going to watch the simulation, and I just want you to observe what is happening—only what is happening, what you see. The second time we watch the simulation, I want you to draw what you see and write down your observations."

Students then watch the simulation, a short video showing subatomic particles moving around the atom and providing a close-up shot of the particles inside the nucleus. After the second viewing, Ms. Warren says, "Now, with your partner, I want you to think of questions you have about the simulation, using your observations. Remember, you are only writing what you saw—don't make any inferences." Ms. Warren invites students at their tables of four to first work with their "shoulder partners," exchanging their questions. They will then share their questions with the other dyad in their groups of four. At one table, José and María work together:

> **María:** For me the question is: because the s- the size is different.
>
> [silence between José and María]
>
> The size color is . . . different.
>
> **José:** The size and color?
>
> **María:** Yes, because the size and color is different. What is YOUR question? Other, other question.

José: No—It's not a question because you have because. It's WHY.

María: Ah! why! Why the size and color is different? For me, is my question. What is your question?

José: Mmm . . . Why (Spanish: *Es que no sé cómo se dice alrededor.*)

María: Round. Round.

José: Round . . . No, no, no, no, "around."

María: Yes, around

José: Why . . .? Wait.

María: Why the—the circles?

José: No, no. Why the atoms are together

María: Why the- Why the- ah, *bueno*. [beginning to write down José's questions]

José: Why the atoms . . .

María: The atoms . . .?

José: ARE together or IS together?—ARE together

María: Is together?

José: I don't know.

María: Is together.

José: Why the atoms is together?

María: Uh . . . other question is, eh, why the electron is there round on the neutron and proton?

José: [inaudible] Why the atom do not have the same, the same, the same

María: No, no, why WHY the the electron is the round, round, round

José: No is my question (*pero*) . . .

María: Is my question, so . . .

José: Is your question?

Ms. Warren: I want you to share your questions at the table. Read your questions to the rest of your table group, and as you read,

I want you to think about just one question. Alright? I want you to decide on one question that you're going to share with all of the class.

As the students enthusiastically work together, Ms. Warren approaches a group and listens attentively to their deliberations. A student asks, "Why the particles is around the atom?" As he speaks, he twirls his pencil to emphasize "around." A second student replies, "Oh, around the other atoms, why is going around the other atoms?" A third student says, "I think, why the electron is smaller than other atoms, and why so faster?" Hearing his question, Ms. Warren asks, "Can you say your question again, please?" He repeats, "Why the electron is so smaller and so faster?" Ms. Warren asks, "How do you know it is an electron?" The boy replies, "Because the electron is smaller, I know this." "But we just had to observe the simulation, it didn't say 'electron' in the simulation, right?" said Ms. Warren. "What did you see?" "Little circles," the student responds. "Right, little circles," echoes Ms. Warren. "Because we don't know yet that it is an electron, we only know we saw little circles. So if you say it's an electron, that is making an inference. We only know now what we can actually observe, right?"

At another table, students in a third group of four share their questions with each other and then start selecting which question they will present to the whole class. Suchada, a girl from Thailand, works with male classmates from Iran, Mexico, and Burma:

Suchada: Is there a structure of atoms?

Asef: What is this?

Ramiro: Why the particles is around the atom?

Farid: Why this little circle, eh, is smaller and, uh, faster?

Suchada: So which question are you—are we—are we going to ask?

Farid: MY question.

Suchada: Let's do this [does "rock, paper, scissors" gesture].

I'm the only lady, so . . . No . . . I'm joking! Or maybe we can join together.

Asef: Yeah.

Suchada: Can do one.

Farid: One. Yeah. My question [finish].

Suchada: No. Let me see. No, we can all join together and just make one/once.

Let me see.

Asef: Why the particle is around the atoms?

Ms. Warren: This table: can you tell me your question, please?

Farid: [sharing the question that puts together the four students' ideas] Why this little circle is smaller and faster and, uh, move around other atoms?

Ms. Warren: That's a big question. Why the little . . . [starts repeating the question]

———————◆———————

What are the major shifts we can see in this vignette? First, instead of learning language as an individual activity, students are engaged in learning as a social process through which they become familiar with science ideas. Second, rather than learning English in terms of grammar and structures, they are learning language as a means to apprentice in scientific analytical practices such as observation and asking questions, and developing scientific language uses. And third, the students are engaged in activities designed to scaffold their development and autonomy as learners.

Now we will elaborate on the pedagogical shifts outlined in table 2.1, describing the changes in practice that each one entails.

From . . . Seeing language acquisition as an individual process

To . . . Understanding it as a social process of apprenticeship

If we took a cursory look at a group of classrooms in American schools today, especially those with a high proportion of ELLs, in the majority of cases we would likely see a teacher standing in front of the room, students seated in rows, tables, or desks clustered together, silently listening to a teacher. Whether or not these teachers consciously hold this view, their actions indicate a belief that learners acquire the academic uses of a second language by listening to someone who knows how to use the language well. A reformulation of practice requires a shift from the view that language learning is something that is internally processed by the student in the brain's "black box" as a result of external input—listening to the teacher. Consistent with sociocultural theory, students' second-language learning is best fostered by participation in carefully structured interactions that provide them with the opportunity over time to develop conceptual understandings, analytical practices, and dynamic language use in a domain.[3]

An optimal way of characterizing this process of participation is apprenticeship. In any field, apprentices learn through being mentored and socialized to become members of a community of practice, for example, a community of lawyers, doctors, carpenters, or weavers. Apprentices are provided with models of their community's practices and opportunities to develop skills, and are encouraged to take risks in a supportive environment so that they eventually appropriate the target skills.[4]

ELLs are no different. They become apprentices in a community of practice focused on specific disciplinary work (math, science, art, history) that entails specific uses of language. Through their apprenticeship in their classroom community of practice, all ELL students can become increasingly skilled in the language use of the discipline.

We saw student apprenticeship in action in Ms. Warren's science class. The students are apprentices in learning an important science practice: asking questions after careful observation of phenomena to seek additional information.[5] They are also developing their understanding of subatomic particles, and they are learning all of this in English, their new language. To support their learning, Ms. Warren has prepared a sequence of steps that take students from individual to group exploration of the meaning of the prefix "sub" through their viewing of, recording observations about, and formulating questions about a simulation video. Students use their own resources, including their native language when appropriate, to make sense of the task. They help each other refine their questions, and they listen attentively to partners' queries. In the culminating activity, teams have to choose one question to be shared with the whole class. After some back and forth, one team decides to combine all of their individual questions into one. In the process, all the students have had the opportunity to meaningfully work on their emerging understanding of concepts and to express them in English.

Ms. Warren has made it possible for each and every student to think, come up with a question, express it, listen to and consider other queries, and finally, working in a group of four, decide on just one question of several offered to be taken to the larger group. In every instance, the process of conceptual, analytical, and linguistic development is mediated by interaction.

Through communicating with peers and mentors, students in Ms. Warren's class gradually and purposefully rehearse their uses of the language, and in the process become increasingly adept at them. Nobody is silent in this class. Every student is provided with the opportunity to be an apprentice.

ELLs also need legitimacy, the recognition by members of the community that, from a shaky start, they have the potential to become full-fledged members of the group. They have the right to engage in ways that may be linguistically imperfect at first, but that nonetheless accomplish the work of communicating key conceptual understandings and processes. We saw the notion of legitimacy exemplified in Ms. Warren's class. Both María and José know that their English is nascent and thus imperfect, but they are both convinced that their efforts are valued and that through them they will become increasingly accomplished at engaging in scientific practices in English. This, they realize, takes effort and perseverance.[6]

From . . . Conceptualizing language in terms of structures or functions

To . . . Understanding language as action

Traditionally, ELLs have been taught how to use the grammatical forms in the language or how to accomplish individual language functions, such as "suggest" or "introduce." However, teaching form and function in isolation from real, meaningful, discourse-based communication has not produced generative, transformative learning for ELLs.[7] Only an emphasis on language as action, which subsumes form and function, engages students in the meaningful learning of new disciplinary practices while simultaneously strengthening their language uses in those practices.

Language as action embraces the idea that, at its essence, language is a tool we use to act in the world. We talk, listen, read, and write to get things accomplished, and we use all language or language-related resources at our disposal: linguistic—language itself; paralinguistic—the intonation, stress, and rhythm that accompany our expressions to signal emphasis or emotional overtone; and extralinguistic—the gestures and body language that mark, amplify, and accompany our remarks. Learners, for example, emphasize their intentions by accentuating elements of their expressions—slowing down, raising their voices, signaling with their hands, using facial expressions such as smiles or frowns. These paralinguistic and extralinguistic features accompanying expression enhance the power and impact of the strictly linguistic elements of communication. When students are in the process of developing these linguistic tools, communication is imperfect, and intonation, repetition, and facial expressions take on added importance.

The students in Ms. Warren's class emphasize their intent for clarification by intoning in interrogative ways, so that "because the size is different" can be rightly interpreted as "why is the size different?" The problem for María is that "why" and "because" sound the same in Spanish (*por qué/porque*). Fortunately in this case, an advantage is that María is from Honduras and José is from Mexico, so they both share Spanish as their native language and recognize the connection.

Whenever the use of their family language is helpful, Ms. Warren encourages students to use it for the benefit of the development of their new language, a practice increasingly advocated in the development of English as a second language.[8] In the careful class grouping, however, students are also required to engage in communicative activity with peers with whom they do not share a language. For example, in María and José's group, one of the students comes from Burma (and speaks Karem) and the other from Iraq (and speaks Arabic).

Language as action emphasizes communication and its impact on language users. This entails using language beyond the production of isolated utterances, emphasizing instead discourse, the verbal interchange of ideas. When José asks his question about why the atoms are together, a discussion of whether the right verb is *is* or *are* ensues before José's question is accepted. Then it is María's turn to express another question, and she asserts her turn in spite of José's interest in adding another question of his own, "No, no, why WHY the electron is there round on the neutron and the proton?" María proposes, but—out of turn—José insists with his question, and María responds, "It is MY question . . ." indicating it is her turn to ask a question.

As we see in José and María's interaction, engagement in discourse takes the form of a to-and-fro between speakers, like tennis players hitting the ball back and forth across the net. José and María's back-and-forth takes them from negotiating an initial idea to negotiating multiple ideas to arriving at some sort of a conclusion. In their brief interaction, we observe how language can both shape and be shaped by its use in particular social settings. It illustrates how naturally occurring interaction uncovers the practices and processes of reasoning by which students make sense of what they are learning.

The nature of the interaction between the students in Ms. Warren's class is possible because she has taught them to pay attention to each other, to focus on what their peers are saying, to "listen beyond accents and errors," and to work hard at making sense of what the other says, improving it if possible. Being deliberately attuned to the other person and what he or she is saying and doing is what sociolinguists call intersubjectivity.[9] As Leo van Lier observed, "[It] is construed as the development of increasingly effective ways of dealing with the world and its meanings."[10] Intersubjectivity leads to mutual respect and to students' efforts being focused on communication rather than on form and function.

From . . . Seeing language acquisition as a linear and progressive process aimed at accuracy, fluency, and complexity

To . . . Understanding that acquisition occurs in nonlinear and complex ways

Most classes for ELLs operate on two erroneous premises: (1) language is learned along a universal progression of linguistic forms; and (2) not correcting student errors (the student knows the grammatical rule but fails to apply it correctly) or mistakes (the student does not know how the rule works, and so his production is ungrammatical) will lead to "fossilization," the inevitable perpetuation of incorrect forms in the student's English. Were teachers to revisit their own experience, or their observations as parents or relatives of babies learning to communicate, they would see that language emerges instead in spiraling ways. To quote van Lier again: "The learner is immersed in an environment full of potential meanings. Those meanings become available gradually as the learner acts and interacts within and with this environment."[11]

As an apprentice in a language community, the toddler initially asks for the cookie she wants by directing her sight to the cookie jar and smiling at her mother. Mother then responds appropriately, "Ah, so you want a cookie," and gives her one. Over time, the child learns to say "cookie," "want a cookie," "Can I have a cookie," and, much later on, "I know I shouldn't have this cookie, but . . . ," inviting reassurance by others. Because the child has apprenticeship opportunities, her range of possibilities to engage in the same requests appropriately across a wide variety of social circumstances gradually increases.

The same process occurs in second-language learning when students are invited and supported to engage in valuable activity, which provides them with practice and the opportunity to develop increasing sophistication in their linguistic uses. Just as the young child learned and practiced language according to the context of the language use, requesting cookies, the sequencing of the language that ELLs learn and practice is determined by the conceptual and analytical development required, not by the assumed complexity of the grammatical forms of the language.

In this vein, let us reflect for a moment on an often-seen practice in American classrooms. How stimulating can it be for second-language learners to be restricted to learning expressions in the present simple tense, or to filling in blanks with the correct form of the verb in the past simple tense in an exercise consisting of ten unrelated sentences? Even worse, based on the assumed inevitability of this sequential understanding of English as a second language, when students do not produce a given percentage of the correct (although meaningless) forms of English in a test, they may have to repeat the same low-level course, and for another semester continue doing the same meaningless exercises that were not helpful in the first place.[12]

It is likely that this pedagogical orientation sustained year after year contributes to the existence of "long-term English language learners" (LTELLs) in middle and high school, those students who have been enrolled in U.S. schools for more than six years who are not progressing to English proficiency. However, the practice of focusing on discrete pieces of language is difficult to counteract, because teachers have developed this habit over many years during the "apprenticeship of observation."[13] The net result of this kind of apprenticeship is often evident in the reactions of other teachers who see videos of Ms. Warren or her colleagues engaged in similar work in other disciplinary areas with ELL newcomers. Many of them comment that the students they watched "cannot be beginning ELLs." Their belief in the sequential development of English tells them that in week 6 of learning English, students cannot yet engage effectively in disciplinary practices, which will necessarily come "after students have more English." Yet, imagine if the pace and excitement of work in Ms. Warren's class were the norm. ELL students might exit the ELL category more rapidly and better tooled!

A number of the same teachers also worry that Ms. Warren does not correct her students' English. What they have yet to realize is that when students are needlessly corrected, they are not only discouraged from developing their ability to participate in academic practices, they are also delegitimized and belittled in their efforts to contribute, as the following example poignantly demonstrates.

In her book *The Spirit Catches You and You Fall Down*, an ethnography of the tragic consequences arising from miscommunication between a California Central Valley medical community and immigrant Hmong refugees, Ann Fadiman relates an incident in a middle school. The teacher had given her class an assignment that required students to describe an autobiographical event. May, a Hmong ELL, wrote an essay about the harrowing experience of her family escaping their home village, walking with small children and babies through territories impacted by a vicious war. May's essay powerfully conveys well-sequenced events, including the abandonment of valuable property the family had started their journey carrying, and sadness and appreciation for the sacrifice made. May's writing is reproduced here exactly as she wrote it:

> My parents had to carried me and two of my younger sisters, True and Yer. My mom could only carried me, and my dad could only my sister. True with many other things which they have to carry such as, rices (food), clothing, and blankets for overnight. My parents pay one of the relative to carry Yer. One of my sister who died in Thailand was so tire of walking saying that she can't go on any longer. But she dragged along and made it to Thailand.
>
> There was gun shot going on and soldier were close to every where. If there was a gun shot, we were to look for a place to hide. On our trip to Thailand, there were many gun shots and instead of looking for a place to hide, my parents would dragged our hands or put us on their back and run for their lifes. When it gets too heavy, my parents would tossed some of their stuff away. Some of the things they had throw away are valuable to them, but our lives were more important to them than the stuffs.[14]

May has used the resources she had developed so far to communicate this tragic and admirable experience. She understands the assignment as an invitation to engage in action and narrate a powerful personal experience. From a communicative point of view, she succeeds. The teacher, however, responds to May's assignment with these comments:

> "You have had an exciting life!" wrote her teacher at the end of the essay. "Please watch verbs in the past tense."[15]

A more appropriate response would have been for the teacher to have expressed her respect and sympathy for May's effort to relate such a painful incident, acknowledging her action. She also errs pedagogically by focusing first on formal aspects of the language, the correct use of the past tense. In fact, one could argue that May has developed an understanding of the rule for the past tense in English (add *ed* to the verb), but her knowledge of the rule is incomplete, so she overgeneralizes it to verbs that do not follow the pattern. Later on, at some point in the lesson, the teacher could have said: "By the way, I see you have detected a pattern in the formation of past tense of verbs in English, that is wonderful. But languages are complicated, and as well as having rules, languages also have exceptions that make learning them difficult. Let us take a look at some instances of exceptions to the rule in your paper . . ."

From May's teacher's actions, we might conclude that she does not have a deep understanding of how the English language works; she fails to see in May's writing the beginning of her development and control of the linguistic system. To ensure May's committed future participation in class and her resulting growth, the teacher would do better to make efforts to recognize her strengths in communicating and to work on building her confidence. Every time teachers engage first in meaning making with students, they develop their interest in communicating and their willingness later on to review their oral and written productions to improve them.

In Tanya Warren's class, we see quite a different response to her students' communicative efforts as she redirects students' performance as it relates to the important elements of the science practices they are learning. For example, when a student draws an inference from his observation of the simulation about electrons, he says, "Why the electron is so smaller and so faster?" Although the teacher's instructions have been to observe and ask questions, Ms. Warren responds, "How do you know it is an electron?" When the student replies, "Because the electron is smaller, I know this," she redirects him: "But we just had to observe the simulation, it did not say 'electron' in the simulation, right? What did you see?" leading the student to respond, "little circles." Ms. Warren's objective is to apprentice her students in the scientific practices of keen observation and of asking questions about the observations. She also wants her students to develop conceptual understandings related to the subatomic particles. In future lessons, they will continue developing their understanding as well as the concomitant language uses.

While we have stressed the language in action approach and the benefits of engaging students in language use in worthwhile disciplinary contexts, occasionally and strategically, teachers can leverage a "language moment," calling attention to a salient feature of language and explaining how it works. Immediately after, the teacher continues work on substantive aspects of ideas and analytical practices for which that specific language is used. In employing this language moment, the teacher is somewhat akin to an orchestra conductor, who may need to isolate the violins to focus on a few bars, and when satisfied that the desired level of playing has been reached, immediately returns the violins to continue playing the symphony with the full orchestra, making the music the composer intended.

Language use spirals in sophistication, depth, and eventually correctness, based on the opportunities students have to use it to express important ideas, and it always develops simultaneously with conceptual understanding and analytical disciplinary practices.

From . . . Emphasizing discrete structural features of language

To . . . Showing how language is purposeful and patterned

All languages are patterned. There is regularity in the way linguistic elements are used to indicate the types of actions speakers or writers want to accomplish, for example, in convincing somebody to use a particular type of product or to leave a bathroom clean after it is used. To illustrate this further, we'll consider the use of persuasion in advertising.

There is a continuum in the degree of force that a persuasive text conveys depending on its use of modal verbs. An advertisement can convey different suggestive pressures depending on which of these statements is used: *You could have multiple admirers if only . . .* or *Be popular . . .* or *You ought to look nicer this summer . . .* ELLs need to understand these differences in order to recognize the impact that language can have on others.[16]

Likewise, texts of a certain type or genre follow similar organization, and use similar expressions. When we hear a colleague say, "Oh boy, what a class I had during my fifth period today . . . ," we expect this to be the beginning of a narrative to give us information, or to entertain us or make a point. We know our friend's story will unpack an event that made the day special for her in one way or another! We also expect that specific events will be linked by words such as *then, after that, suddenly*. This understanding of the social function of texts, their organization, and typical language enables speakers or readers to orient themselves to the act of communicating. For example, whenever students hear "How are you?" from somebody they do not know well, they should recognize that the other person is being friendly and greeting them. They should also know that only certain responses, such as "Fine, how are you?" or "I'm doing well, thank you" are appropriate. They should know that saying "Today is Monday" or "I am feeling terrible, I have a bad headache and I didn't sleep very well last night," while grammatical and even factual, are inappropriate responses to the question asked.

The same is true of written texts. For example, short stories and essays are very different types of texts, and in each of these genres their purposes determine their linguistic features, which make them immediately recognizable. If ELLs are taught to identify the nature of texts, their communicative purpose, and their typical organization and characteristic expressions, they will be able to free their attention to focus on the novel elements of the text. For example, an ELL student in an elementary school is helped to recognize that the phrase "once upon a time" introduces a story. She also learns that story structure involves a character, a setting, and that something happens to the character (the plot). She will also expect to hear or read transition statements that describe the sequential action in the story: *then, after that, suddenly, meanwhile.* Finally, she will know that in the end something will happen to resolve a situation in happy or unhappy ways. Recognizing the "landscape" of the story and the expressions usually used to move the action forward helps her concentrate her efforts on making sense of the novelty in the story—how this story is different from (and similar to) others she has heard or read before.

The predictability that comes from knowledge of story elements and expressions is essential for ELLs' understanding of the genre's communicative purpose and organizational pattern, and assists students in recognizing what tends to come first and what follows in the ideas presented.

Similarly, when ELL students encounter a taxonomic report, one that classifies items into classes or types, they need to understand that the purpose of these texts is to organize some area of knowledge according to a class-subclass categorization or a part-to-whole arrangement. They also need to know that structurally these texts usually begin with a general statement whose purpose is to classify and define, and that they then name the classes as a macro theme. Students need to be aware that what occurs next is a description of subclasses and their distinctive characteristics, with the addition of parts and functions of each component. In terms of language, ELLs need to know that taxonomies include definitions of technical terms, classifiers and describers in noun groups, generalized participants, "timeless" simple present tense ("It rains a lot in Portland"), relating verbs (be, have, seem, appear), a topic as a theme, general-to-specific organization of information within paragraphs, and no time sequence.[17]

As another example of an opportunity to develop students' understanding of language patterns, in beginning courses, students could learn how to understand the purpose and organization of a text by perusing it first and learning to notice key details, such as, does the author say he is going to tell a personal story, describe a process, or explain why something is valuable? They could also focus on the words that link ideas. For instance, do the students find words that refer to sequences, such as *first, then, after that*? If so, this is a clue that the text may contain instructions or be the narrative of an event.

Students could also learn that many words used in disciplinary texts look similar in English and in Latin- or Greek-derived languages, such as Spanish. For example, cognates, words that look alike in two languages and share the same meanings, are recognizable in print, although they are pronounced differently. *Structure* and the Spanish word *estructura* look similar, as do *composition* and *composición*, so the chances are that they refer to the same concept. Students need to see the words in Spanish and English to be able to identify them as cognates and assume they mean the same thing in both languages. Since a discussion about cognates and their exceptions conducted in English would be too complex for students at the beginning level of proficiency to understand, the explanation about cognates could be given in their native language if the teacher speaks it. For example, if the teacher speaks Spanish, using this language may be helpful to most students, given that the highest percentage of ELL students in U.S. schools speak Spanish as their family language. What teachers say, even those who speak Spanish, needs to be carefully prepared with the help of specialists, so that students are provided with a script that neither overexplains nor does not accomplish its purpose. These explanations should initially be given to teachers in writing to help them offer students the "just-right" kind of information, no more and no less. An example of such a script is:

Miren, muchachos, hay palabras que en inglés se llaman *cognates*—en español, "cognados." Estas palabras se ven muy similares tanto en uno como en otro idioma si estos derivan del griego o latín, y tienden a ser palabras importantes en el desarrollo de prácticas disciplinarias. Cuando lean un texto, revísenlo para ver si encuentran *cognates*, porque pueden serle muy útiles. Por ejemplo, *composition* y *composición*, *relevance* y *relevancia*, y *structure* y *estructura* son cognados en inglés y español.[18]

Many students, however, come from homes where languages other than Spanish are spoken. In this case, teachers could engage speakers of those languages from the community in preparing translations, which may be written or recorded.

With such activities, students beginning to learn English are able to develop understandings that are typically not expected of students at early levels of proficiency in their second language. In contrast, when students focus on discrete formal language knowledge, they do not develop academic skills and language awareness that will be transferable. Emphasis on discrete pieces of language does not lead to generativity; instead, students' language skills remain inert. Over time, metalinguistic skills, such as the ability to recognize types of texts by concrete indicators, are practiced in English and appropriated, while other disciplinary practices become the focus of apprenticeship in English.

Knowledge of the patterns of language is essential not just to orient second-language learners through their work in a language they are beginning to control, but also to help them grasp the most important rules of the system and gain confidence in their use of the language. Recognizing patterns leads students to feel more in charge of their own learning—to be able to use language across contexts and to develop their agency as learners.

From . . . Using lessons focused on individual ideas or texts

To . . . Using clusters of lessons centered on texts that are interconnected by purpose or by theme

This shift focuses on the promotion of deep learning as a core goal of the college and career ready standards. Specifically, the shift is characterized by a selective focus on the essential elements of a concept or theme, their interconnections, and student engagement in higher-order thinking.[19] Teaching that progresses atomistically from one discrete point to another and does not weave in the relatedness of concepts or themes or help students understand the structure of knowledge in a domain leads to superficial, shallow understandings that are not useful for generating new understandings. Deeper learning is achieved when students are supported to link ideas into constellations of understandings that are interrelated. This type of knowledge is robust and generative. When students develop clusters of understandings, also known as schemata, they are better able to generate new learning, since these preexisting mental structures serve as anchors for building and organizing new knowledge.

No two students are alike, and the development of disciplinary practices in English will occur at different paces for each of them. When constructing learning experiences for ELL students, it is important for teachers to keep in mind that the more conceptually connected lessons and units of study are, the more productive the joint enterprise of learning will be for all. This is because, when teachers develop specific ideas and themes in iterative, deepening, and expanding ways, students will be able to move at their own pace from peripheral understanding to an increasing command of conceptual understanding, analytical practices, and language. If all students in a class, progressing at different rates, center on the same rich and generative conceptual, analytical, and linguistic practices, they will be able to interact with each other meaningfully and assist each other's growth, in spite of their different levels of understanding and language use.

◆

Interconnectedness Fosters Deep Learning

The following example presents the way in which a teacher, in a very different context than those so far explored, uses learning connected around an idea to advance her students' practices in English. Later on, we will see how at one moment in a lesson she uses students' personal knowledge to anchor their investigation of brain injury and the consequences it has for individuals. The example comes from Ms. Crescenzi's class at Lanier High School in Austin, Texas.

But first, before we examine what is happening in the classroom, it is important to add a note about the class and its purposes so we can understand the power of the pedagogy the teacher uses. The course Ms. Crescenzi teaches used to be called the Remedial English class, but she has now renamed it The Psychology Seminar. This relabeling is part of an effort Ms. Crescenzi has made to signal important shifts in her own understanding of how to work with students and make them legitimate apprentices in academic practices. Most of the students in her class are LTELLs, and many were born in the United States.[20] They have not been effectively assisted in their acquisition of the academic uses of English or in acquiring the knowledge and analytical practices that make schoolwork successful. As a consequence, they are "struggling readers" and, in attempts over two or three years, have not passed the writing test, a prerequisite for graduation in Texas. Students such as Ms. Crescenzi's are often characterized by schools as lacking skills and motivation.

Ms. Crescenzi decided to restructure her course content and pedagogy, transforming what used to be formal, teacher-fronted lessons that covered isolated units of language and writing into lessons that explore a variety of psychological issues through interrelated ideas that have appeal to teenagers. Her renovated classes embed ample opportunities for students to talk, read, and write as they apprentice in conceptual and academic skills as well as the oral and written academic uses of English. She now realizes that if an idea is explored through multiple lenses, iteratively deepening key understandings, students will gradually develop not just more robust knowledge of the ideas, but also the skills and language needed to apply this knowledge in critical and appropriate ways in the future. Furthermore, she knows that these invitations, if appropriately scaffolded, will engage students, motivating them and eventually helping them succeed in and beyond this specific task.

In this five-period lesson, students work through a jigsaw. Ms. Crescenzi has carefully structured the project with the aim of developing practices leading to students writing a compare/contrast essay. First, students meet in groups of four (the base group) to prepare for reading some texts. In their base groups, students activate their prior knowledge by sharing personal experiences relevant to the focus of their exploration, brain injury and its potential consequences. When they have shared their experiences, they study and discuss two diagrams: one pictures the brain and its components; the other, a chart, explains the different parts of the brain, its structures, functions, and what may go wrong if the brain is injured.

On the second and third days of the project, each member of the base group joins a different group of four (the "expert" group), with whom they will interactively read and discuss a case of brain injury, becoming the experts on their particular case. Ms. Crescenzi has deliberately constructed the groups to challenge and support them at their level of development as they read and discuss the texts. As a result of this careful planning, during their expert group time, students will be developing metacognitive skills and will be helped to see that they can develop "intellectual stamina," the ability to sustain attention on an academic task that is difficult and learn what to do when they read texts beyond their comprehension.

One of the texts is about the case of Cheyenne Emerick, a young snowboarder who suffers an injury during a descent from a mountain, causing him terrible daily seizures.[21] The other three cases present the stories of a former soldier with a brain tumor, a victim of an industrial accident, and a young woman who suffers seizures and hallucinations following a blow to the head. To signal important information, which will then be shared back in their base groups, the teacher gives all students the same four questions to address while working through their texts:

- Who suffered brain injury?
- What kind of accident was involved?
- What part of the brain was compromised?
- How did the injury impact the victim?

Of importance, these texts have been differentially engineered. The text about the Cheyenne Emerick case is a complex and high-interest story with key conceptual development opportunities for students. It is also the shortest text, comprising five pages. Ms. Crescenzi intensely engineered the text by dividing it into sections, providing subheadings and focus questions after the subheadings, along with textual elaborations and pictures that explain new terms. The students in need of the most support will read this text.

The second text, based on the case of Charles Whitmore, is six pages long. Ms. Crescenzi engineered this text less intensively. For example, the Emerick case has five photographs, with captions that elaborate critical elements depicted in the pictures (e.g., one picture shows a snowboarder flying in the air, and the caption reads, "A snowboarder's dream is to soar through the air, flying high above the snow"). The Whitmore case contains only three pictures and uses fewer elaborations because it relates a story that is bound to be familiar to some students in class, as the incident narrated happened in Austin, where the students live (i.e., a mass shooting from the University of Texas at Austin's main tower, which is depicted in one of the pictures in the text). She has moderately engineered the other two texts, which are seven and eight pages long, respectively, providing fewer textual expansions and only one picture each. Students in need of the least support will read the text whose only photograph has no caption.

After the reading is completed and answers are agreed upon, the students in each group write a summary of their learning on a chart. Then groups are reconstituted back to base group formation so that the four different cases are represented in each base group. Students share their responses in their groups. As homework, students are asked to read independently a second case in order to write an informational essay. The teacher plans to introduce and model this essay structure on the fourth day of the project.

While almost invisible accommodations have been made for their different levels of proficiency in English and in reading, working collaboratively all students know that their piece is equally important, and they hardly notice the differences in difficulty of the texts. This is one example of how a conceptually connected lesson that includes sustained discussion enhances the possibilities all students in a class have to develop—and also to support their peers' growth of—deep understandings, analytical skills, and sophisticated language use.

———————◆———————

From . . . Engaging in activities that preteach content

To . . . Engaging in activities that scaffold students' development and autonomy as learners

We conceive of scaffolding not merely as help provided to students to assist them in completing a momentary task or to preteach the content of a text, but rather as supports specifically designed to induce students' participation in meaningful and worthwhile activity while developing and increasing their autonomy. Drawing on Vygotsky's notion of activity in the "zone of proximal development," Wood, Bruner, and Ross have suggested scaffolding as a metaphor for the "just-right" kind of support that teachers provide to move students beyond their current state of development.[22] Consistent with the aims of college and career ready standards and deeper learning, the goal of this kind of support is to make students' knowledge generative, or transferable, so that they can use it in the future to support new learning on their own.

Scaffolding is always responsive to what teachers observe about students' current development and is designed to advance their learning. Pedagogical scaffolds, just like the physical scaffolds used in the construction of buildings, should be constantly changed, dismantled, extended, and adapted in accordance with the needs of the workers. Neither the scaffolding used in construction nor the pedagogical kind has value in and of itself. When teachers provide scaffolding, they construct support to begin where the student currently is, so as to allow the student to build on and accelerate development. Thus scaffolding is proleptic, or forward looking.[23] Its job is not only to help the student be successful at a task, but to develop future skills. In the words of Leontiev, a Russian psychologist who worked with Vygotsky, the goal of work in the zone of proximal development is to help learners become as soon as possible who they are not yet.[24]

Scaffolding comprises two key elements: structure and process. The structure, just like in a building, is there to provide security to workers and to make construction possible; scaffolding supports work that would otherwise be impossible or dangerous. Similarly in a classroom with ELLs, the scaffolding teachers design presents students with participation structures, formulaic expressions, and other supports that enable their safe participation in academic activity that can then be carried out increasingly in English. We have seen scaffolding at work in the vignettes in this chapter. The process, the work the students do, encompasses what the students can accomplish with the supports the teacher provides them. From this perspective, scaffolding learning may begin with tasks that allow for students' agency and initiative, assisting them to develop autonomy.[25] The tasks are structured carefully in ways that neither lead to chaos nor stifle the learner's development. Participation made possible by scaffolding, as in the case of Ms. Crescenzi's students, enables the emergence of novelty and revelations about students' lives. During the process, teachers need to be observant in order to decide whether new supports are needed to enrich or accelerate students' evolving understandings and autonomy.

From . . . Establishing separate objectives for language and content learning

To . . . Establishing objectives that integrate language and content learning

There has been a tendency for ELL teachers to state the objectives of a lesson separately as language objectives and content objectives. This tendency leads to dichotomous pedagogical approaches, which, because they are not integrated, are unlikely to result in knowledge that can be transferred across situations.

A further problem with ELL teachers stating two types of objectives for their lessons is that the duality suggests a sequential approach: you first need language in order to acquire the concept and the analytical practices. In this view, learning concepts and analytical practices is conceived of as the integration of discrete understandings learned independently of language. In this regard, for example, one often hears mathematics teachers say, "You (the ESL teacher) teach them English, I will then teach them mathematics." Instead, mathematics teachers need to conceptualize mathematics learning as apprenticeship into mathematical disciplinary practices. This is the case not only for those who teach mathematics, but for all subject matter teachers.

Apprenticeship underscores the process of gradual learning, enhancement, refinement, and deepening of ideas and analytical practices and of the language required to express them. In Tanya Warren's class, we saw that students were simultaneously learning about subatomic particles, learning how to make observations and raise questions, and learning the English required to convey it all. While the students' analytical practices are still emerging (accomplished scientists would not express themselves in the ways that these students do), with continued engagements in learning language, ideas, and practices simultaneously, the skills will become increasingly sophisticated and transferable.

From . . . Using simple or simplified texts

To . . . Using complex, amplified texts

Research and practical work on text complexity has often focused on identifying features that make particular texts more complex than others, matching readers to appropriate texts, and simplifying texts with the intention of supporting comprehension and reading development. However, if texts are matched to a student's ability to handle them, how are growth and development promoted? As we discussed earlier in this chapter, learning needs to take place in the student's zone of proximal development, more recently referred to as the construction zone.[26] This metaphor refers to the area that lies beyond a student's ability to act on his or her own, where socially mediated learning prompts development. How teachers design, organize, and enact their teaching is pivotal to this development. However, teachers need to be assisted to develop the skills such as Ms. Crescenzi used in scaffolding highly complex texts to make them more accessible to ELLs so that they could both develop their communicative abilities and overcome otherwise overwhelming comprehension difficulties.

In this respect, it is important to differentiate complexity, difficulty, and accessibility.[27]

- **Text complexity.** This dimension has traditionally been measured in terms of word and sentence length, and sentence structure. Assuming that a word is more complex because it is longer is misguided, especially for students whose family languages have Latin or Greek origins, since many long academic words are cognates: *estructura, structure; diagonal, diagonal; complementario, complementary*. Equally misguided is the assumption that for an ELL a longer sentence is more complex than a shorter one. Sentences are typically made longer by the presence of connectors. Phrases such as *in spite of, consequently, on the other hand*, and *contrary to what was expected* connect ideas in meaningful relationships, and once students learn the relationship the connector introduces, they are assisted to understand key aspects of the sentence. Rather than making understanding simple, depriving sentences of these connectors obscures meaning. The intention of making texts simpler actually results in the text becoming more unintelligible, as you will see in the simplified version of the fable "The Turtle and the Hare" in the next chapter.

- **Text difficulty.** This criterion concerns the relationship between a reader and a specific text; for example, how much does the reader know about the topic, theme, or ideas in the text the teacher is considering using? Does the reader enjoy or know something about the topic? More familiar topics will make reading easier for ELLs, while new topics will make reading in English more difficult.

- **Text accessibility.** As we saw in Ms. Crescenzi's class, accessibility for ELLs depends mostly on the pedagogical scaffolding provided by teachers. Within second-language research on text engineering, a tension exists between providing students with original, "authentic" texts that pose possible comprehension difficulties and choosing or creating simplified texts, which may not always ease comprehension burdens, and will, in fact, limit language-development opportunities. Three decades ago Widdowson drew a distinction between *simplified texts* and *simple accounts*: "A simple account is a genuine instance of discourse, designed to meet a communicative purpose," while a simplified version "is not genuine discourse," but rather "a contrivance for teaching language."[28] For example, simplified versions may alter the text according to purely language-directed rules, such as "simplifying a sentence by creating two sentences if the original statement includes two ideas." In this case, "Pedro had already had breakfast, but when he smelled the pancakes Jane made, he could not resist her invitation to have some" becomes "Jane made pancakes. Jane invited Pedro to have pancakes. Pedro ate some pancakes."

Simple accounts clarify referential meaning, for example, pronouns that refer to names introduced earlier on in a text. They also clarify prepositional meanings, phrases introduced by a preposition that establish relationships such as in the example above. "But when" alerts the listener—or reader—that what is going to follow will be somewhat contradictory to the prior statement "[he] had already had breakfast." These elaborations aid comprehension.

ELLs need to learn with simple accounts because the use of simplified texts does not prepare them for academic practices. Examples of a simplified version and of a simple account created at the sentence level are shown below:[29]

> **Original sentence:** Because he had to work at night to support his family, Paco often fell asleep in class.
>   **Simplified version:** Paco had to make money for his family. Paco worked at night. He often went to sleep in class.
>   **Simple account:** Paco had to work at night to earn money to support his family, so he often fell asleep in class the next day during his teacher's lesson.

The above examples are for illustrative purposes: ELL students need to learn with simple accounts of complete texts. For example, Ms. Crescenzi engineered the complete texts her students discussed to include a number of features that made them more accessible than the originals. Chunking the text and inserting explanatory pictures, elaborations, and headings that alert the reader about what may come next enable students to access the text. This kind of text engineering supports students in accessing complex ideas and sophisticated concepts through reading.

From . . . Teaching traditional grammar

To . . . Teaching multimodal grammar.

As college and career ready standards note, with the increasing prevalence of digital texts or hybrids, which combine traditional and digital texts, it is important that students extend what they are learning about the reading of written texts to visual and electronic texts. For example, ELLs need assistance in understanding how texts privilege space, size, color, and other elements as means of communication. As we saw earlier in the advertisement examples, there are multiple techniques used to "sell" products with different degrees of intensity, from "soft" to "hard" sells. The same deliberate increase or decrease of intensity can be manipulated through the use of visual and textual elements.

Consider, for example, how visual elements such as figures common in one context can be transposed to unfamiliar contexts to highlight the intended message. In the same way that good writers may break the rules of grammar for impact, creators of visual texts may transpose images to create a desired impact. For instance, a Hot Wheels (toy cars) advertisement shows a child's bedroom. In the bedroom, a traffic policeman is giving a contrite child a ticket, presumably because the child was "driving" (pushing) his toy car too fast. In the picture, the policeman's figure is at the center and is enlarged, while the child appears to his left, small, head down, hands behind his back. The picture plays humorously with the notion of authority. The Hot Wheels logo appears at the bottom right of the picture, almost too small to see. However, the message—Hot Wheels cars go fast—is not diminished because of the smallness of the logo—quite the opposite, the "grammar" of the picture highlights its impact.

In another example, an advertisement for the World Wildlife Fund presents a picture of the deep sea with a vertical line dividing the picture in half. In the first half, a shark's fin slices through the water's surface. In the second half, we see a smooth and calm sea. The first half is labeled "Horrifying," and the second half is labeled "More Horrifying." What message is the picture conveying? A superficial reading leaves viewers thinking that it is more horrifying not to know whether there is a shark hidden under the water in the second part of the picture. However, students need to understand that, when reading (or listening to somebody), it is important to know who originates the text, what we know about the creators of the text and the purposes they are trying to accomplish, and what impact they want to have on us—for instance, the acts they may want us to carry out: believe, buy, or vote. Given that this is a picture from the World Wildlife Fund and we know that its members have as their mission the protection of habitat, we can conclude that its message is that it is more horrifying not to have any life in the ocean than to have some sharks living in it.

In the same way that accomplished users of language "act" persuasively because of the way they construct their messages, so do users of multimedia texts. ELLs need to be invited to explore these forms of communication and their intentions in order to be able to respond appropriately.[30]

From . . . Using tests designed by others

To . . . Using formative assessment

Formative assessment may be described as a process that guides the design and enactment of learning opportunities from moment to moment. As such, it is the contingent hallmark of pedagogy, and in recognition of its importance, we will explore this last shift in full in chapter 4. That discussion will also dispel the prevalent notions of "formative assessments" as products that can be written generically, published, and used in schools. Formative assessment is an active and organic outgrowth and director of learning.

In this chapter, we have detailed the reformulation of practice for ELLs needed to achieve the challenge of the college and career ready standards. In the next chapter, we will examine the theories that underlie traditional approaches to the education of ELLs, and more contemporary theory that undergirds the pedagogical shifts we have described in this chapter.

CHAPTER 3

———————— ◆ ————————

From Theory to Practice

*Examining Assumptions About Language
Acquisition, Learners, Learning, and Teaching*

I n chapter 2 we presented some major pedagogical reformulations required to provide ELLs with quality opportunities to engage in deep, generative learning. At its best, teaching is a highly intellectual act, and as such requires that teachers constantly examine the theories that guide their work and analyze the resultant practices. While many teachers think of themselves as practical and removed or uninterested in the theoretical world, in reality they all have theories that consciously or unconsciously guide their teaching. If teachers are going to successfully engage in reformulations of practice, they first need to gain awareness of their current theoretical stances and any inherent limitations therein. Only then will they be in a position to transform their existing theoretical perspectives and the teaching practices on which they are based. In this chapter, we will explore some of the theories that have historically informed ELL teachers' thinking, the understandings that inform their practices, and the reformulations of practice that arise from current theory and research.

The traditional approach to the education of ELLs has been that specialists teach English as a second language while grade-specific or subject matter teachers teach them content. However, as we saw in the prior chapter, there is little conceptual growth that does not entail language development, and little language learning that does not include conceptual and analytical skills development or enhancement.

To begin our exploration of how theory drives practice, we present two vignettes drawn from observations in beginning ESL classes. The first vignette takes place in a high school after students have been in English language learning classes for a full semester. The second, also in a high school, occurs after students have been in an American school for six weeks.

Vignette One: Reconstructing "The Turtle and the Hare"

Students in this class are seated at tables of four, seemingly arranged into groups that share the same native language. The teacher, Mr. Caldera, announces that the class will continue their work on the fable "The Turtle and the Hare," which they have read the day before.[1] Mr. Caldera has written the objectives for the day on the board:

Content objective: Explain a story

Language objective: Retell a story using key words and signal words

Vocabulary: Character, setting, conflict, resolution

Mr. Caldera gives each group a set of pictures from a children's book and some strips with sentences printed on them. He asks the students to reconstruct the story by organizing the pictures and sentence strips. The sentences on the strips are simple and do not include connectors or transition words. The students, for the most part silently, play with the pieces and arrange pictures and statements. The statements (in order here) are: The race begins in the forest. / The rabbit is very fast. He runs past the turtle. / The rabbit sleeps. The turtle walks quietly. / The rabbit stops to talk to girls. / The turtle does <u>not</u> stop to talk to girls. / The rabbit plays sports. / The turtle walks fast to try and win the race! / The turtle wins the race! Some brief discussion occurs among the students, mainly in their native languages. Their discussion shows some confusion:

Anita: ¿El conejo habla con chicas? girls? No entiendo [the rabbit talks to girls? girls? I don't understand].

Charo: Me imagino que son estas conejas . . . [I imagine they are girl rabbits (pointing to the picture)].

The teacher walks around the class observing what the students are doing, but he doesn't intervene. After approximately fifteen minutes, Mr. Caldera asks students to read the text their groups have put together:

Maritza: The race begEEns in the forest. The rabbEEt sleeps. The tOOrtle walks quietly.

Mr. Caldera: BegIns, rabbIt, TErtle. Please repeat after me.

Maritza: BegEEns

Mr. Caldera: BegIns

Maritza: No puedo, BegEEns

Mr. Caldera: Does another group have a different version? Anybody?

Gabby: The turtle wins the RAIse. The rabbEAt sleeps . . .

Mr. Caldera: RAIse, rabbIt. Please repeat.

Gabby: RAIse, rabbet

Mr. Caldera: Anybody else?

Although Mr. Caldera keeps looking for the correct answer, in fact, he directs his attention to correcting students' pronunciation rather than providing guiding feedback. Not having received the expected answer, he writes the correct version of the text on the whiteboard and asks all the students to copy it in their notebooks. When they have done this, he has the students read the text aloud after him, one sentence at a time. In the last five minutes of class, Mr. Caldera asks students to discuss what the story is about. Most students speak in their native languages and are not talking about the fable. Finally, Mr. Caldera asks for someone to share his or her summary, but students do not volunteer responses, and since time is running out, he concludes, "This is the story of a race between the hare, who is a rabbit, and a turtle, and in the end the turtle wins."

◆

Vignette Two: The Clarifying Bookmark

Robert Thompson is teaching his beginning ESL class at the International Newcomer Academy High School in Fort Worth, Texas. (We have already encountered students from the same school in Tanya Warren's class in chapter 2.) Students are going to read a narrative that Mr. Thompson has engineered because he thought the original text in his textbook was superficial and almost stereotypical. The story, which is told from the perspective of an American girl on an organized student visit to Washington, DC, describes her initial misunderstanding of and eventual friendship with a Muslim student also on the trip. To prepare his students for reading the text, Mr. Thompson introduces them to a modified version of the clarifying bookmark shown in figure 3.1 and explains how to use it.

> The section of the first page is called "A Trip to Washington, DC." There is a question there. It says, "Why does the writer go to Washington, DC, and what does she do there?"
>
> So, as you read this, I want you to try to get the gist of what you are reading. When I say "get the gist," I mean get the main idea. You may not understand every word, but you'll get a general idea of what's happening.
>
> We are going to read the first page using the clarifying bookmark. Partner number 1 may "get the gist" of what she's read. Maybe you understand and can summarize what you've read. So, if you understand and summarize what you've read, then you will say (using a prompt on the clarifying bookmark), "I understand this part, and I can summarize it by saying . . . ," and in your own words, you'll tell the main idea of that paragraph.
>
> Partner number 2 is going to respond. Partner number 2 can respond either by saying, "I agree with your summary, and I can

FIGURE 3.1 Clarifying bookmark

I am going to . . .	What Partner 1 can say . . . 	What Partner 2 can say . . . 
 Summarize what I read	I can summarize this part by saying . . . OR I think the main idea of this part is . . .	I agree with your summary, and I can add . . . OR I disagree with your summary because . . .
 Ask for clarification	This part confuses me a little, because I don't understand . . . OR I'm not sure what this is about, but I think it might mean . . .	Yes, I can help. I think this part means . . . OR I am confused about this part, too, because . . .
 Use prior knowledge to help me understand	I know something about this from . . . OR I have read or heard something about this when . . .	This also reminds me of . . . OR I think the main idea of this part is . . .

add," and maybe say some additional information that you can add to the summary, or maybe you disagree with the summary, and you explain why you disagree.

Nirmala, a Nepali girl, works with Cristina, a Mexican classmate:[2]

Nirmala: I go to read the last paragraph. [Reading]

> *During the week in Close Up I learned a lot, I had a lot of fun, and I saw in one week more important places than I had seen during my whole life. I loved the Lincoln Memorial and the Washington Monument. I was impressed by the beauty, elegance, and quietness of the Library of Congress. The museums were wonderful and they did not cost anything to go in, they were free!*

> What I can say is I understand this part, and I can summarize it by saying she feel exciting because she learn a lot, many, many things, and also was very funny. She to know many place that she don't know. And also she loved the Lincoln Memorial and the Washington Monument, and all things that she visit was free.

Cristina: I agree with you, Nirmala, your summarize and I can add during the week in Close Up she learn a lot and she have a lots of fun. She saw important places. Now I am going to read. [Reading]

> *A program called "Close Up" selected students to go to Washington, DC, the capital of the United States, for a week. I was very lucky, really fortunate, to be one of the students who went on this program. For me it was very exciting to go from Fort Worth, Texas, to one of the most beautiful cities in the country, where there were so many important places and things to see. In Washington, my classmates and I studied about American government, we visited important buildings and monuments, we attended sessions of Congress, and in general we learned a lot about history and government.*

> OK, I am going to ask for clarification. This part confuses me a little because I don't understand "Close Up selected" who

select? select students? they go to Washington DC? in our school we have this program?

Nirmala: Yes, I can help. Students have good grades, they go to DC. We ask Mr. Thompson later. Right?

Mr. Caldera sees as the goal of his instruction that students gain the ability to produce grammatically correct sentences in English. It is also important to him that his students pronounce the sentences they are reconstructing into a text as closely to the standard as possible. The text he uses, however—a simplified version of the original—is not an example of a well-formed story or fable. It lacks the elements that characterize the genre: a clear social purpose, a sense of dilemma and resolution, clearly demarcated reasons and sequences, and a lesson to be derived from the story.

Mr. Thompson, on the other hand, is mainly concerned that his students understand key aspects of the text they are reading: how one student visiting Washington, DC, learns not only about the nation's capital, but also about the diversity and sameness in human beings. Furthermore, he combines learning English with learning how to read critically, emphasizing the understanding of key ideas in the text while developing students' awareness and tolerance of what they do not understand. The text, which he engineered to substitute for the impoverished text in his textbook, contains complex sentences and also abundant elaborations intended to help make the reading more accessible. Mr. Thompson is not initially preoccupied with grammatical or pronunciation accuracy. Rather, his first focus is on the conceptual understandings and critical reading skills that his students develop as they engage in uses of English.

From these two vignettes, we can conclude that Mr. Caldera and Mr. Thompson's respective teaching practices emerge from quite different theories. In figure 3.2, we show four types of theories that influence teachers' classroom practice: second-language acquisition, learning, learners, and teacher understanding. These theories combine to provide an integrated (although at times not always coherent) theory of learning and teaching

FIGURE 3.2   Theories influencing teacher practice

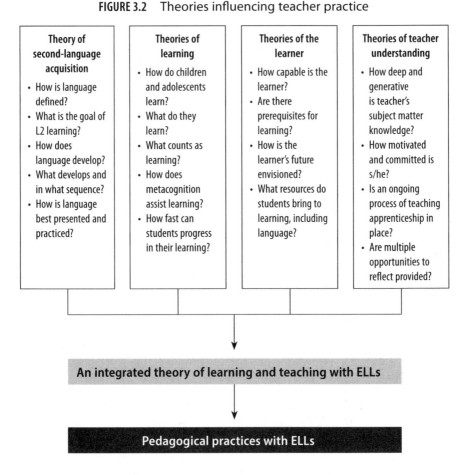

that influences the pedagogical practices of ELL teachers. When teachers are aware of the theories they operate under, they can describe what they do, explain why they do it, say what outcomes they anticipate from their pedagogical moves, and explain results—or the lack of them.

Where do Mr. Caldera's and Mr. Thompson's two very different approaches to teaching English come from? We are now going to examine in more detail the ideas that generated them.

Theories of Second-Language Acquisition

EMPHASIS ON TEACHING LANGUAGE AS FORM

Formal theories of language, which led the field for centuries until the 1970s, define language as composed of specific forms to be learned, for example, sounds, vocabulary, and sentences. Turning the second-language learner into a version of the idealized native speaker was regarded as the goal of instruction. This perspective on language learning led to the development of two approaches or methods: grammar-translation and audio-lingualism.

GRAMMAR-TRANSLATION METHOD

Implemented for centuries, this approach used the masterworks of literature as the basis for learning the patterns of language, or grammar. It assumed that the writers of the classics knew best how to use the language, and so these texts were the focus of language learning. Students had to study grammar rules and memorize lists of vocabulary through repetition. In these classes, the use of students' native languages was necessary because learners applied their knowledge of vocabulary and grammar to the slow and careful translation of the classics to their first language. Although few elements of the grammar-translation approach are still present in schools today, its focus on lists of words, grammar, correctness, and authority, and on written language as an object of study rather than of use, has survived, notably in Mr. Caldera's class, where his concern was correct pronunciation and correct grammar.[3]

AUDIO-LINGUALISM

This approach, which became very popular in the 1950s, conceptualized language as patterns structured into three systems: (1) the phonological system, focused on the sounds of the language; (2) the morphological system, focused on words; and (3) the syntactical system, which addressed grammar at the sentence level. These systems were the focus of teaching and learning. For example, the highly influential Lado/Fries method had a red book, a blue book, a green book, and a yellow book that were used separately in ESL classes, one each for students' study of the grammar, the sounds, the vocabulary, and the usage (through contrived dialogues and sentences) of the three systems listed above.[4]

Typically, an audio-lingual class would begin with a dialogue that students needed to repeat after the teacher as closely as possible to the model. The dialogue contained several examples of the grammatical form to be taught. Because the same grammatical patterns had to be presented many times in a brief exchange, the dialogues were contrived and inauthentic. Oftentimes students had to memorize and perform dialogues in class, giving rise to the name "mim-mem" method (for mimicry and memory). Teachers immediately corrected students' mistakes, fearing that the wrong usage might become automatic. And because native speaker-like pronunciation was paramount, pronunciation, intonation, stress, and rhythm were emphasized, as these were essential to developing a good accent.

In addition, a portion of class time was dedicated to the practice of sounds that would be problematic for students (based on a contrastive analysis of the sounds of their first language and English). For example, Spanish speakers would have drills that emphasized minimal pairs. An example of such a drill is: seat/sit, eat/it, read/rid. Students engaged in these repetitions following the teacher's model, and were followed by the teacher's reinforcement. Many times they did not understand what they were saying, the intended goal not being meaning, but correct pronunciation. More ambitious practices set the target sounds in sentences: Sit on the seat; Eat it.

Also, teaching for habit formation included substitution and mechanical transformation drills, for example, changing isolated sentences from the present to the past tense. Teaching also included completion drills, in which students were required to fill in blanks in sentences with the correct form of the verb.

A consequence of the audio-lingual approach was that oral language—listening and speaking—became the central skill in second-language teaching, with relatively less emphasis on reading or writing. The selection and ordering of what was to be taught followed a purported sequence moving from simpler to more complex structures, and from vocabulary items and expressions that were supposed to be more immediately useful to those that were less relevant. This sequencing was assumed to follow natural developmental patterns in the second language. Teachers needed to closely follow procedures dictated to them by the materials. This requirement signaled to teachers that no specialized knowledge was needed to teach language, and the notion that native speakers were ideal second-language teachers gained currency.

Several components of the audio-lingual approach still influence language teaching today. Many current ESL curricula, courses, and teaching practices reflect the view that language teaching progresses along universal paths; that is, all students need to learn the second language by following the same formal progressions that lay foundations as prerequisites to purportedly more complex combinations.

The belief also persists in language instruction that the native speaker is the model to which students should aspire, and fearing the consequences of learners' imperfect productions, teachers influenced by remnants of audio-lingualism continue to correct learner errors as soon as they occur. Finally, many policies and programs still value adherence to a curriculum above teacher expertise, maintaining the view that teachers should teach prescribed materials in lock-step fashion, focusing their efforts at the sentence level, and should not deviate from plans created by outside "experts."

Within formal theories of language, repetition and memorization of models, sounds, words, and sentences were considered essential to learning. The goal of language teaching was the acquisition of a system that would not necessarily be essential to people's lives or studies.[5] While students' native languages were indispensable in the grammar-translation method, they were deemed problematic in audio-lingualism, since their use was believed to interfere with the development of English. Within the audio-lingual view, the only elements of importance were grammatical correctness and a good accent.

Clearly, what students require today in the context of new standards is to engage in discussions that transcend the sentence level and involve them in discourse. These requirements go beyond work guided by formal approaches to second-language development.

Mr. Caldera's class exemplifies the shortcomings of formal language-learning approaches. The sentences he is working with—part of the curriculum adopted by his district—are all simple sentences in the present tense. We infer that the assumption of the curriculum writers was that this choice would provide opportunities for students to develop the basics of the language without unnecessary confusions. The opposite ends up being the case. Because the text is all in the present tense, students do not understand that events happened in the past and in a sequence, a confusion that is aggravated by the lack of connectors (*such as, first, then, after that, suddenly*) that could clearly mark the sequence of actions in the story. In fact, the whole purpose of the fable is to teach a lesson, and animal characters are used only to illustrate human virtues and follies. However, the nature and function of fables, the features of the characters involved, and the consequences of their actions are all missed because of a preoccupation with the form of language. When we consider Mr. Caldera's approach, a nagging question arises: at what point will students be ready to tackle sophisticated new English language development and college and career ready standards?

Mr. Thompson's class presents a very different learning environment. His students are engaged in exchanges where the exploration of ideas is central. Mr. Thompson has engineered the text not to simplify it in accordance to grammar rules, but to amplify it. Mr. Thompson does not feel that he has to use the materials available to him in the school; he trusts his developing knowledge of how to orchestrate active and powerful lessons. As we will discuss later, his class follows a very different orientation to language and pedagogy, one that privileges student engagement, collaboration, and focus on the growth of ideas, thinking skills, metacognition, and the language needed to communicate them appropriately, although not yet grammatically. We can assume that Mr. Thompson's students will be in a position to develop the content knowledge, analytical practices, and the language competencies called for in English language development and college and career ready standards.

In the next section, we consider cognitive theories that have impacted teacher practice.

Theories of Learning

COGNITIVE THEORIES

A major theoretical change in the study of language came about in the mid-1960s, heralded by the linguist Noam Chomsky. While Chomsky was not interested in the application of his theoretical work to teaching, his ideas influenced second-language teaching nevertheless. Below we describe his unintended contributions to the second-language teaching field.

Chomsky proposed that the study of language was concerned with the study of competence, the tacit knowledge that native speakers have about the rules of their language that enables them to produce and understand the sentences of a language. Although focused on first-language acquisition, Chomsky's work triggered significant changes in the field of second-language teaching. Some of these changes included a move away from emphases on habit formation and drilling, as we saw in the audiolingual approach, and toward the idea that students will automatically derive rules of language from exposure to it.

In 1957, Chomsky published *Syntactic Structures*, in which he developed the idea that each basic sentence in a language has two levels of representation: a deep structure and a surface structure.[6] The deep structure represents the core semantic relations of a sentence. Chomsky theorized that these deep structures generate the surface structures of actual sentences that communicate meaning through a process of transformation. Chomsky believed that these deep structures were similar across languages, but that when deep structures were realized as the surface structures of actual sentences through transformations, they did this differently across languages. For example, negative transformations that turned affirmative sentences into negative ones are realized in distinct ways. For instance, in Spanish and English the negative comes before the main verb: *Yo NO voy*, I do NOT go; in German the negative goes at the end of the sentence: *Ich gehe NICHT*, for example. Two main approaches to teaching second languages were developed within this tradition: the natural approach and learning strategy theory.

NATURAL APPROACH

During the 1970s and 1980s, building on Chomsky's notions of language learning as knowledge of rules that develop in the minds of users in universal ways, Krashen, and later Krashen and Terrell, an applied linguist and a second-language teacher, respectively, developed an approach to second-language acquisition and teaching based on five hypotheses:[7]

- **Acquisition-learning hypothesis.** This proposes that learners acquire the structures of second languages subconsciously as a result of exposure to the second language.
- **Monitor hypothesis.** This hypothesis states that consciously learned language can help students to check, correct, and refine their performance, but with the caveat that such monitoring slows down the learner's production.
- **Natural order hypothesis.** This hypothesis stipulates that learners acquire the rules of language in a universally predictable way that is not influenced by what is taught and does not necessarily follow an order of increasing formal complexity.
- **Input hypothesis.** This states that the best way to acquire a second language is by being exposed to language that is one level higher than the student's current proficiency.
- **Affective filter hypothesis.** This hypothesis emphasizes the importance of a nonthreatening environment for learning, proposing that an "affective filter" (a metaphor) is raised when students are made to feel anxious or stressed, thus eroding a student's possibilities of learning. To promote language acquisition, teachers should lower the affective filter by creating low-anxiety environments.

Krashen's ideas have significantly impacted ESL pedagogy, with repercussions still felt in the field. These pedagogical practices include:

- Teachers' uptake of his caution to avoid raising the affective filter. This has sometimes translated into "not pushing students" and not asking students to focus on how they express their thoughts in the second language, since the concern should be on learner fluency (being able to speak easily, at normal rates of speech, without hesitancy), not necessarily on learner awareness, which would slow down learner production and affect fluency.
- The widespread use of the comprehensible input concept. This involves the teacher presenting simplified language models that add one increment of complexity to students' existing language (the oft-quoted i+1).[8] However, because this construct was never operationalized, it was difficult to find agreement on what it really meant. For

example, some teachers thought that their speech to students should be limited to one verb tense that had not been studied in class, while others thought they should use no more than a small number of words students did not know. However, what was clear to everyone was that simplification by teachers was required.

- A dominant belief among teachers that because listening to comprehensible input triggers language development, the students do not necessarily need to be actively engaged in talking in class. As a result, many teachers today still believe in the importance of offering students simplified input and of using texts that have been stripped of their linguistic (and conceptual) sophistication as the sole requisite for students to develop their second language.
- Acceptance of the notion of "the silent period." Krashen proposed this as the initial stage of second-language acquisition, wherein students should not be expected to produce, because they are still in a "pre-production" stage. Many teachers use this idea to explain why their students are not asked to talk in class yet, or why beginning-level ELL students are not expected to actively participate in productive group work.

If we review Mr. Caldera's teaching, and May's teacher's approach in the excerpt from *The Spirit Catches You and You Fall Down* in chapter 2, we see many instances of the influences of the formal and cognitive theories of language. Among these are the idea that sequencing simpler sentences will lead, after students learn or acquire them, to the development of increasingly complex ones; a preoccupation with correctness; and a focus on language production that is controlled, as opposed to developing meaningful, stimulating, or transferable language.

LEARNING STRATEGY THEORY

Cognitive views of language also produced a very different line of linguistic work. While a strong emphasis on the conscious monitoring of linguistic activity was not desirable in Krashen's view, a group of applied linguists, influenced by Chomsky's ideas, proposed learning strategy theory. In this view, learners deliberately apply cognitive techniques to their second-language learning to control their linguistic performance, overcome difficulties and problems in the second language, and enhance their results.

Building on these ideas, several taxonomies of "teachable" learning strategy theories appeared in the field.[9] The best known of these is the Cognitive Academic Language Learning Approach.[10] Teachers, however, found its proposed classification of strategies complex and difficult to use effectively in classroom settings. Additionally, from young students' perspectives, the exclusively metacognitive focus of the proposed work was unappealing. However, we do believe that a deliberate focus on metacognitive strategies is immensely useful in the education of ELLs when it is combined with a focus on interaction and meaning making in accordance with proposals contained in the new standards. Examples of their positive impact can be observed in Robert Thompson's class in this chapter and in Stacia Crescenci's class in chapter 2, and again later in this chapter.

In the late 1970s, there was a revolutionary shift in the way language was defined and studied both at the theoretical and applied levels. Claiming that the most interesting and pivotal aspect of language was understanding the rules that governed its use, and how this use changed across contexts, sociolinguists proposed that linguistics should focus on the study of how language functions in society. Functional theories have had an immense impact on second-language learning, and are also reflected in new standards for English language proficiency. We elaborate these theories below.

Functional Theories

Within this theoretical perspective, language is defined as a tool speakers use to carry out specific social acts, or functions, in ways that are appropriate to the specific societal environments in which interactions occur. For example, if we need to request some salt at the dinner table, our expression will vary depending on the situation. With our spouses, it may be enough just to move our heads in a certain way to signal we need the salt, or simply say, "Salt?" In a formal dinner we may say either "Would you pass me the salt, please?" or "Can you, please, pass me the salt?"

In this hypothetical example, the speaker is issuing a directive. If a second-language learner were to reply, "Yes, I can," and do nothing, he would not be making sense of the social function of the utterance, which goes beyond the form through which it is expressed. Form and function in this, and many other cases, vary across circumstances. For example, "Would you open your books to page 67?" is a directive and not a question. As such, the expected answer is definitely not "No, I wouldn't."

To further illustrate the complexity of what is said and what is done linguistically, we excerpt a brief exchange from Stacia Crescenzi's class during the brain unit. Having read, discussed, and taken notes on the individual stories each expert group read, students now go back to their base groups and begin sharing the information with their peers. In the following exchange, Carlos, Rosalía, Julián, and Roberto work together. Ms. Crescenzi joins them for a while.

What they say (form)	What they accomplish (function)
Carlos: His story was the beginning, it was the beginning . . .	*Starts the report*
Rosalía: Why is this person famous?	*Tries to hurry through the task*
Carlos: The story was the beginning of the story, of the story . . . of the biological basis of behavior.	
Rosalía: Oh! Are you serious? Hold on, this doesn't sound right.	*Requests clarification*
Carlos: His story was the beginning of THE STUDY of the biological basis of behavior. Okay, biological basis of behavior.	
Rosalía: Ok, what happened to this person that caused brain impairment?	*Hurrying report*
Carlos: A stumping rod may have penetrated Phineas Gage skull.	

What they say (form)	What they accomplish (function)
Roberto: Did you put that he got that little thing through his head, right? (makes a gesture as if his finger was going through the head)	*Restating information and trying to avoid using sophisticated language*
Julián: Yeah.	
Roberto: Awesome!	
Julián: The rod. The rod may have penetrated	
Roberto: Do you have to use a big word like that? I'm just gonna put "went through."	*Restates his lack of willingness to use specialized language*
Julián: Why don't you put *p* and then a dot?	*Making fun of Roberto's laziness*
Roberto: There's a name for that word . . . the part that was injured. She said . . .	
Rosalía: And damaging both frontal lobe, frontal lobe according to . . . What were the areas of the brain that were damaged? . . . (addressing her group) I keep spelling it "lube."	
Julián: What was the third question?	
Roberto: Hold on, we got to let her (pointing to Rosalía) catch up.	
Rosalía: I'm still on number two (taking the notes from Carlos).	*Not letting Carlos copy notes.*
Ms. Crescenzi: (joining the group) Ah, ah, ah, no.	*They have to be presented.*
Carlos: No? I have to read it to them?	*Confirming directions*

What they say (form)	What they accomplish (function)
Ms. Crescenzi: Yes.	
Carlos: Aw.	
Ms. Crescenzi: He can read it and he can spell things. And he's very good at this.	
Rosalía: Why can't I just copy it?	
Ms. Crescenzi: It doesn't help you practice the language. Doesn't help *him* practice the language. I want you to be able to use these academic terms.	
Rosalía: But I KNOW English.	*Protesting*
Ms. Crescenzi: Yes, but *psychological* English.	
Carlos: But we don't speak English very well.	
Ms. Crescenzi: Ah, begin . . . (signaling Roberto)	
Julián: It's not his story though, it's his (pointing to Carlos).	
Ms. Crescenzi: Ah, then Carlos you need to do it.	
Carlos: Okay. The rod . . . The rod may have penetrated Phineas Gage's skull.	
Ms. Crescenzi: Right. The rod penetrated his skull.	
Julián: The rod. Okay. Okay, and then what else?	*Trying to derail the work with a protest*

What they say (form)	What they accomplish (function)
Carlos: His personality changed and he became mad easily.	
Rosalía: I don't like this.	
Ms. Crescenzi: It's O.K.	*Acknowledges Rosalía's protest*
Carlos: Ah! He became mad easily . . .	
Julián: Because his personality changed, he became mad easily.	
Carlos: He became mad easily.	
Ms. Crescenzi: Good. Who's gonna go next?	*Takes the opportunity to hurry the process*
Rosalía: I'll go next so I can finish.	
Ms. Crescenzi: Ok, not a problem.	

We can clearly see the form of language that students are using and the specific function of its use.

The focus on the function of language use arises from the work of Michael Halliday in the United Kingdom and Dell Hymes in the United States, among others.[11] Inspired by this work, many sociolinguists in this tradition began to focus not on structural forms or idealized competence, but on the social use of language, or performance. In sociolinguistics, the variation in performance is examined as a product of social context and social constraints. And in applied linguistics, the development of communicative approaches to second-language teaching reflected this new understanding of language.

Sociolinguists proposed that variation was governed by rules: speakers of a language agreed what was appropriate and followed these social patterns to avoid being inappropriate. In addition to the idea of "grammatical competence" (the ability to produce the grammatical sentences of a language) arising from Chomskyan linguistics, sociolinguists developed the notion of "communicative competence" (being appropriate in a specific social context), the idea that language use is normally fitted to and appropriate for particular social contexts. Communicative competence was viewed as emerging from participation (and socialization) in different contexts and the different patterns of language use that are appropriate to them.

Sociolinguists' study of the function(s) of language, what speakers accomplish when they say something—such as requesting information, praising, suggesting, and so on—took precedence over the study of linguistic forms. We see this emphasis reflected in Tanya Warren's class. When, after some deliberation, María and José agree to state their question as "Why the atoms is together?" Ms. Warren not only lets the question go without correction, but she actually acknowledges its validity. In this way she validates the action they are engaged in as appropriate to the context, while knowing that there will be future opportunities to work on *is* and *are*. At this point, she is happy that the students are making sense of the assigned task, appropriately participating in the activity, and enjoying it because they are learning.

Second-language teachers influenced by this tradition moved from an emphasis on correctness (accuracy) to a focus on appropriateness, in which the primary emphasis was on the student's ability to fashion language that was appropriate for particular communicative purposes. Initially, however, a limitation was that, in ESL classes, the pedagogical approach was a focus on one function at a time. For example, teachers worked on *requesting* information in one lesson, and in the next lesson on *suggesting*, treating communicative acts as fulfilling only one function. While immensely promising in theory, the implementation of the communicative approach emphasized the atomistic treatment of communicative functions, a limitation that mirrored past inadequacies of formal approaches.

Three main strands within functional language teaching merit highlighting because of their potential for pedagogy that addresses language, content, and analytical practices learning represented in the new standards.

ENGLISH FOR SPECIFIC PURPOSES (ESP)

This approach focuses on the design and teaching of courses to develop well-defined competencies based on an analysis of the uses of English that students will eventually need for school and work. Having a clear idea of who the learners are, what they know, and what they need to do in English became essential for the design of syllabi and curricula and pedagogy.

ESP courses challenged a number of assumptions about the teaching of English. For example, classes intended to develop the second language in well-defined contexts (English for Reading Engineering Texts, for example) could be carried out partially in students' mother tongues. The sequencing of what was to be taught in the English class depended on the need to understand specific elements of texts; for example, how cause/effect relationships are typically expressed in engineering texts. In this case, the formal or the cognitive assumption that there was an order in which languages were acquired became unimportant, since the progressions of what was to be learned needed to be determined by its usefulness to specific learners. Although these ESP approaches have not been highly influential in K–12 settings to date, they nonetheless offer K–12 ESL teachers useful ways of thinking about the selection and progression of curricular content, with language need and usefulness determining what is taught.

Another idea adapted from this work is the pedagogical value of employing students' first language in classes where students and the ESL teacher share the same language, a context that is common, though far from universal, in American schools. We saw an example of this in Ms. Warren's class, where students were using their native language to support their development of English.

COMMUNICATIVE LANGUAGE TEACHING

Communicative language teaching emphasizes the learner's ability to carry out communicative functions (acts) in the second language by talking in ways that are appropriate for specific communicative contexts; for example, participating in conversations with friends that involve requesting, explaining, sustaining ideas, and responding to requests for elaboration. Teachers who adopt a communicative language teaching approach emphasize their students' fluency, or ease of use, in the second language as they carry out these functions in particular contexts, and they regard issues of accuracy, or correctness, as secondary.

We have seen an example of this approach in Mr. Thompson's class when Nirmala and Cristina work together on a text to increase their reading skills, to understand a text that is beyond their current level of comprehension, and to develop the language required to carry out this work. As they apprentice in the uses of English, their exchanges are not grammatically correct, but they are felicitous and they communicate what needs to be accomplished.

Another positive consequence of communicative language teaching, with its emphasis on interaction, has been the acceptance of learner error and a validation of students' hesitations and reformulations as necessary steps in the process of developing communicative abilities in the second language.

SYSTEMIC FUNCTIONAL LINGUISTICS (SFL) APPROACHES TO SECOND-LANGUAGE TEACHING

Michael Halliday proposed that texts do not have meaning—they have the potential for meaning. He argued that meaning is realized in the act of interaction, whether in face-to-face interaction or the interaction of a reader or viewer with an author, mediated by a text. Halliday's work in accounting for the meaning potential of texts led him and others to develop a functional perspective to language teaching that linked grammar to meaningful functions (for the most part in written text).[12] This move paralleled other British linguists' efforts in the late 1960s and 1970s to design a system of categories based on the communicative needs of the learner in which function dictated the language the learner needed to use. Teachers whose pedagogy is based on SFL focus on explicitly teaching language forms as meaning-making resources for both first- and second-language learners.

In the American context, systemic functional linguist Mary Schleppegrell has explored "the linguistic features of the language students need to learn for success in school," with the understanding that this new emphasis will help both ELLs and speakers of nonstandard varieties of English to develop disciplinary uses of English.[13] For example, Schleppegrell uses SFL analyses to contrast how grammar is used differently to make meaning in texts in specific disciplines.[14] In addition to utilizing specialized vocabulary, disciplinary texts use different grammatical resources to encode meaning, to signal interpersonal dimensions (interpretations, attitudes, and judgments), and to organize coherent messages. For example, science texts use noun groups to categorize terms and processes, create theory, construct reasoning, and link ideas in text. Scientific texts also use specialized technical vocabulary, nominalization (e.g., turning *sensitive* into *sensitivity*) to deal with abstraction, and dense clauses in tightly knit language, increasing informational load. History textbooks tend to use clause structures to signal "interaction of time and cause and the foregrounding and backgrounding of interpretation." In mathematics, students must manipulate long and complex noun groups to solve word problems. Students in language arts encounter multiple language patterns in literary and informational texts designed to "entertain, divert, challenge, and educate."[15]

The following example shows an analysis Schleppegrell carried out using SFL to explain how historical texts change across the grades, become increasingly dense and abstract, and in the process lose many other important meaning signals. The sentence is from an eleventh-grade text:

> The destruction of the buffalo and removal of Native Americans to reservations emptied the land for grazing cattle.

As Schleppegrell observes:

> To explain what the dense sentence means, a teacher would need to unpack it in more or less the following way:
>> Settlers and hunters killed all the buffalo, and the government forced all the Native Americans to leave their lands and move to reservations. Because the animals and people who had lived on the plains were gone, the land was available, so ranchers began to raise cattle.[16]

SFL approaches help students understand how meaning relates to agency (who performed specific acts), logical connections (the meaning relationships among words and phrases), reference (the use of pronouns to refer to people introduced before), and interpretation (how meanings are assigned to statements). These dimensions are presented in the grammatical as well as lexical features of texts at different levels.

If we return to Schleppegrell's example text, we can see that agency has been deleted. Who or what caused the destruction of the buffalo? We are not told. Who removed the Native Americans? It is not mentioned. The text has eliminated clear causal links such as *Because* in the second sentence in the second text. Teachers can gain important insights from SFL about how texts progress linguistically across the grades that can help them determine which texts they will use and how.

A few questions are worth asking about the use of SFL in American schools: To what extent does explicit attention to textual meaning-making devices need to be elaborated in school? In what dosages? And for what purposes? What level of teacher understanding is required to engage in this work powerfully, generatively, and compellingly? Undoubtedly, the contributions that SFL offers teachers are invaluable, but important knowledge for teachers does not necessarily translate into that knowledge being of equal importance for students. In our experience, this fine knowledge about language, which Halliday and his colleagues developed working with teachers in Australia over more than three decades, does not exist in the United States. In fact, even in Australia, this knowledge is not general among all teachers.[17]

Another perspective that has influenced approaches to teaching and learning for ELLs comes from sociocultural theory. We turn to that next.

Sociocultural Theories of Language

More than eight decades ago, Vygotsky proposed seminal ideas that have been accepted and developed by psychologists and educators all over the world for the last three decades. Two main ideas from Vygotsky influence second-language teaching and learning: (1) language mediates all human action, and (2) learning is an essentially social process of co-construction in the zone of proximal development, defined as the area beyond what the learner can do independently, but where actions can be accomplished with the assistance of more able others.[18]

The idea of language as a mediator and the notion of scaffolding as co-construction of learning provide ELL teachers with guidelines for their pedagogical approaches with ELL students. Sociocultural theory proposes that students learn language as apprentices in meaningful interaction.

Taking this view to the classroom, second-language teachers need to design structures and opportunities for students to engage in scaffolded interactions with the teacher and their peers. Over time, participation in interactions helps students develop content knowledge and communicative abilities.

A major difference in sociocultural theories of learning from previous ideas of what develops when students learn is their perspective on language-teaching approaches, which promotes the integration of conceptual, analytical, and linguistic development. Central contributions of this perspective include the notion that apprenticeship through meaningful activities moves students from peripheral to central participation (or appropriation) over time, and that scaffolding that is contingent upon the emerging strengths and needs of the learners is required to do so.[19] The impact of sociocultural approaches to teaching can be seen in the growing emphasis on the importance of pedagogical scaffolding and classroom interaction to facilitate language development.

The formal, cognitive, functional, and sociocultural theories described above have impacted U.S. ESL teaching in K–12 schools to varying degrees in recent decades, and their legacies are reflected in curricula and classroom pedagogies. In addition to theories of second-language acquisition, teachers' practice is also shaped by their theories of the learner, as is shown in figure 3.2. In the next part of the chapter, we explore this component of integrated theories of teaching and learning for ELLs.

Theories of the Learner

Learning and teaching are not the same across contexts. Good teaching, which triggers productive learning, is always situated in the particular. While the same principles of learning (for example, promoting academic rigor for all students; holding high, clear, and actionable expectations; engaging students in quality, sustained interactions; focusing on language whenever that focus is warranted) may apply across contexts, their particular instantiation will always be different.[20] This is because teachers are very different individuals, and so are their students.

Teachers' views of the learner impact how they treat their students, the invitations they offer them to participate and grow in their learning, and the specific supports they provide to support learning. These views are influenced by societal assumptions. Sometimes teachers have to engage in "unnatural acts" to challenge these assumptions and develop more productive understandings about second-language learners.[21]

An example of these assumptions about learners that must be questioned is the differential societal appreciation second-language learning has in American classrooms. In the late 1970s, Joshua Fishman proposed the idea, further developed by Guadalupe Valdés in the early 2000s, that a second language, one that is learned after the first language is established, could be learned either as a foreign language (FL) or as a second language (SL).[22] In the first case, the student's native language is valued as much as the foreign language and is not in danger of disappearing as a result of studying the second language. At the same time, the required levels of proficiency to be acquired in the target language are not very demanding, since the language is not indispensable to the individual's functioning in society. When students study a SL, however, the target language is indispensable, since participation in society is predicated on its use; an individual's first language is threatened by the development of the second language and is seldom appreciated in this environment. Fishman said these differences lead to two different types of bilingualism, which he called "folk" and "elite," while Valdés addressed them as "circumstantial" and "elective." Table 3.1 outlines these two perspectives.

In American schools, ELLs are children or teenagers who not only need to learn the English language, but also must learn literacy skills and disciplinary academic practices in English at the same time. They have to do so in situations where, as outlined in the below chart, they are minority students with all the tensions that that condition entails. On the other hand, postsecondary students, on whom most of the research has been conducted, have quite different needs. They typically have been highly educated in their countries of origin and have already developed strong literacy and subject matter content skills in their native language. They now need to learn a second language to express and expand these practices at the tertiary level. In the case of FL instruction contexts, learners are studying English as an added advantage to their education, but they will not be studying academic subject matter in an English-speaking environment, and do not need the language as the mandatory medium of

TABLE 3.1 Two different sociolinguistic situations in second-language learning

A sociolinguistic look at L2s	
Foreign language (FL)	Second language (SL)
• Student does not need it to interact fully in country of residence	• The language is required for effective civil participation
• Standards for proficiency are quite tolerant	• Standards for proficiency are very demanding
• The L1 of the student is valued and unquestioned	• The value of the student's L1 is not appreciated by many
• The FL does not displace the L1	• Over time, L1 is displaced by L2, with severe consequences
• Leads to "elite," or "elective," bilingualism	• Leads to "folk," or "circumstantial," bilingualism

instruction and learning. Consequently, the subject language for them is of a general, not disciplinary, nature.

Pressures to develop the level of competence needed in the second language of school-age students are not comparable with these situations. For example, in the United States, ELLs are expected to perform on par with native speakers and take high-stakes tests using English, while students of a foreign language are not tested in disciplinary course work undertaken in the second language. In fact, for the most part, they do not study subject matter courses in the foreign language. Consequently, after four years of study, American students of foreign languages reach the equivalent of the American Council of Teachers of Foreign Languages' levels of novice-high or intermediate-low, a situation that would be unacceptable for ELLs.[23]

Another example that explains the differential view of ELLs in American schools relates to their use of their family language. We saw that formal understandings of second-language learning eliminated the use of students' native languages because of a fear of negative transfer. However, Ms. Warren's class presented a very different perspective, one that valued what the students brought to the classroom, especially their family languages, as fertile ground to be used for the construction of new under-standings, skills, and practices.

The last decade has witnessed developments in linguistics and applied linguistics that challenge deep-seated assumptions in the field of English-language teaching. These developments contest the notion of "native speaker–like" knowledge and performance as the goal of language instruction. As we saw in the examples of Mr. Thompson, Ms. Cardenas, and Ms. Warren in their apprenticeship process, their students do not initially produce correct utterances, although they may be engaging in socially and functionally appropriate interactions.

In a more globalized society, the prevalence of only one dialect of English and its pronunciation is being contested. Indian, Chinese, and Latin American Englishes are being perceived as being as appropriate as Boston or Middle Atlantic Englishes. Thus, students' accents, while malleable to improvement, are accepted in this new global reality. In this context, the important considerations are: Are the rules of use being respected? Do students understand the nature of text and the purposes of interactions, and can they respond appropriately?

New understandings of linguistic knowledge and performance also challenge the view of bilingualism as the sum of the mental competence and proficiency of two monolinguals; that is, the competence of the first language user plus the competence of the second language user. In this sense, the notion of "translanguaging," the fluid use of communicative (including linguistic) repertoires—for example, strategically moving between one's first and second language—is gaining currency in the field.[24]

Theories of the learner also include ideas about how capable the learner is and whether there are prerequisites for his or her learning. For example, does the learner need to first construct grammatical sentences before he or she can participate in deep learning of disciplinary practices? Mr. Caldera clearly thinks that, unless students can construct grammatically correct sentences in the present simple tense and pronounce them well, they will not be able to work with texts that contain other tenses. Because texts are seldom constructed within specified linguistic constraints (Dr. Seuss's books for children are a wonderful exception), this prerequisite eliminates the possibility for ELLs to engage in disciplinary work that is grade level.

Sheltered instruction is an example of this minimization of the expectations placed on students. During the mid-1980s and continuing until now, sheltered instruction courses were proposed for subject matter teaching. In these classes, students were sheltered from the complexities of English, while the expectation was that they were still learning subject matter content. The following example illustrates one practice promoted in sheltered classes. The original text has been simplified for ELLs (see our discussion in chapter 2), and the students have to fill in the blanks.

Original text:
Describe two situations in which the medieval knight wore his armor, and tell how the armor he wore was specifically suited to that situation.

For English learners:
Medieval knights wore different armor for different situations. For parades knights wore _____. This was good because _____. For tournaments, knights wore _____. This was good because _____.[25]

The vignette of Ms. Cardenas's classroom in chapter 1 presents the opposite view from sheltered instruction courses. Ms. Warren and Mr. Thompson share her expectations of their students. They do not take the view that it is indispensable to control the language input students are presented with. All three of these teachers are more concerned about the appropriateness of student participation, having them communicate in evolving language, and engaging them in worthwhile activity that will build deep and transferable conceptual understandings, analytical skills, and dynamic language uses.

In the final section of the chapter, we examine the fourth theoretical field shown in figure 3.2, which helps inform teachers' integrated views of learning for ELLs.

Theories of Teacher Understanding

Research on teacher education and teacher development has evolved considerably during the last three decades, and has focused mainly on what teachers should know and do.[26] The dominant paradigm for teacher knowledge that prevailed for a long time viewed teaching as a "process-product" model, focused on the particular behaviors of teachers that resulted in increased academic achievement for their students.[27] Policy stemming from this perspective promoted research on teacher competencies that ended up reducing the complexity of teaching to a set of testable behaviors. As a consequence, a fixed understanding of teaching emerged, one that failed to account for the ways in which teachers help students learn disciplinary content in specific settings.

In opposition to this mechanistic and fixed view of teaching, Shulman offered a conceptualization of teaching as grounded not in particular behavioral patterns, but in pedagogical reasoning. Shulman proposed the concept of pedagogical content knowledge, "that special amalgam of content and pedagogy that is uniquely the province of teachers, their own special form of professional understanding."[28]

In addition to pedagogical content knowledge, Shulman identified other categories of knowledge that together constituted a knowledge base for teaching: (1) subject matter knowledge (deep understanding of their discipline); (2) pedagogical knowledge (general knowledge about teaching that cuts across subject areas); (3) an understanding of curriculum and other "tools of the trade"; (4) knowledge of learners; (5) knowledge of the specific context in which learning is to be promoted; and (6) knowledge about the purposes of education.[29] Shulman argued that the professional expertise of teachers also encompasses a cycle of pedagogical reasoning and action that draws on these knowledge categories, resulting in dynamic expertise and reflective practice.

Shulman's influence on the conceptualization of knowledge for teaching has been immense, especially his notion that deep subject matter understanding, while necessary, is not sufficient for accomplished teaching. Paralleling this notion, expert speakers of a language do not constitute good teachers of that language merely by virtue of speaking or even knowing about the language. Teachers must transform their subject matter knowledge so that students can understand disciplinary content; design and enact various high-leverage strategies to engage students in subject matter learning; make formative and summative assessments of student learning; respond contingently to students' current learning statuses; and reflect on the lesson and its outcomes.

Walqui built on Shulman's model and adapted it to the education of ELLs, adding, for example, the notion that subject matter knowledge included knowledge of the disciplinary uses of language. Similarly, pedagogical subject matter knowledge included knowledge of how to engage students in the simultaneous development of conceptual understandings, analytical practices, and the language required to express them.[30]

Integrating Diverse Theories

How do teachers put together their understandings about second-language acquisition, how youngsters learn, theories about the learners they teach, and theories about the nature of their own learning and understanding? This enormous and consequential task needs to be valued and supported. However, American teachers have very few opportunities to formally grow on the job and to evolve the multiple ideas that are often superficially presented to them into coherent integrated theories of teaching and learning. We will discuss this problem and how it might be resolved in chapter 6.

Teachers receive too much "strategy" training with little or no reflection of reasons, purposes, moments, and places in lessons where these strategies may be productive. As Lewin observed, "There is nothing so practical as a good theory."[31] It is through theoretical reasoning that teachers become more in control of their practice and can bring coherence to their teaching.

Three of our scenarios present teachers who are aware of the theories that guide their practice. In their lessons, students' current skills, the challenges posed, and the supports provided are all in equilibrium.[32] Their pedagogy has coherence. Mr. Caldera, however, does not seem to understand why he engages in some pedagogical moves. For example, his students are seated in groups of four, but nevertheless work individually. By contrast, Ms. Cardenas, Ms. Warren, and Mr. Thompson are convinced that knowledge emerges dialogically, and they consider their role as constructing engagements and inviting students to interact with each other following certain routines. This scaffolds student performance temporarily, enabling students to focus during reading on what they can understand, as well as helping them to learn to tolerate ambiguity. When, as a result of this support, students gain autonomy at targeted practices, pedagogical scaffolds are dismantled to allow the setting of new targets for learning and new scaffolds, in a spiraling motion that helps the students deepen and extend their understanding and their agency.

Pedagogical coherence merits greater attention in the field of teaching ELLs. Teachers who use strategies learned here and there, which may come from different and incommensurable paradigms, work at cross purposes that lessen the possibility of achieving the desired outcomes for students. Working at cross purposes like this has the same effect as people who want to lose weight picking and choosing elements from multiple diets—they are unlikely to achieve their desired results either!

With the pedagogical coherence that comes from an integrated theory of teaching and learning, teachers can provide quality learning for ELLs that will help them to meet the new standards. In the next chapter, we turn our attention to the assessment practices that teachers employ with their students so as to engage them in contingent teaching and learning.

CHAPTER 4

———————— ◆ ————————

The Role of Formative Assessment

Putting Content, Analytical Practices,
and Language Together

J ust as current theories of second-language learning stimulate different pedagogical approaches to better serve ELLs, contemporary ideas
about assessment in the service of learning result in different assessment approaches than the ones that have prevailed in the United States
throughout the last century and into the twenty-first century. The prevailing assessments, which have been dominated by professional psychomet-
rics, are rooted in theories of learning as knowledge acquisition. These
learning theories privilege passivity in learning rather than the active
creation of knowledge through participation in a community of learners.
The notion of assessment reinforcing a passive stance to learning is well
captured by Peter Elbow when he observes:

> People think of listening and reading—not talking and writing—as the
> core activities in school . . . If we stop to think about it, we will realize
> that students learn from output—talking and writing . . . Notice, for
> example, how many teachers consider assessment or testing as measur-
> ing input rather than output. Tests tend to ask, in effect, "How well have
> you learned others' ideas?"[1]

As we saw in previous chapters, while ELL students certainly need to listen to and read English, they learn the language by using it, mainly through talking and writing. Consistent with developments in sociocultural learning theory, ELLs must be active learners who co-construct knowledge of content, as well as language capabilities, through dialogue with their teachers and peers.[2] When learning is viewed in this way, it ceases to be a commodity that is acquired, and instead becomes a continually developing capacity for each learner.[3]

Any assessment method needs to be congruent with ideas about learning.[4] Within a view of assessment that supports students as active constructors of knowledge and language whose learning is in continuous development, value is placed on interaction between students and teachers and among students. In this context, assessment is understood as a social act.[5]

If we return for a moment to the vignette in chapter 1, we can see how assessment as a social act operates. Recall that Ms. Cardenas's students are researching desert cactuses. Throughout their study, the students engage in dialogue to develop and share ideas and provide each other with feedback. As a result, Ms. Cardenas has ample opportunities to listen in on their conversations, noting how they are using language and where she might intervene in the moment to scaffold language use, as well as to identify any language aspect she would like to address with the individuals, groups, or the whole class at a subsequent opportunity.

Similarly in chapter 2, we saw Ms. Warren's students engaged in dialogue during their science investigation that supported their learning of content and analytical practices. As she listened to their interactions and asked questions, she could obtain evidence of both their thinking and their language use. Both teachers' assessment practice takes place within the social acts that occur in the "flow of activity and transactions in the classroom."[6]

Essentially, the form of assessment that both these teachers engaged in is at the heart of pedagogy. It is assessment as a pedagogical decision-making process, not a measurement process.[7] A measurement process is intended to measure achievement in learning. In other words, what performance levels students have achieved after a more or less extend period of learning. End-of-year assessments, interim/benchmark assessments, and classroom summative assessments are examples of assessment as a measurement process. These types of assessment and their purposes will be discussed further in chapter 5. In contrast, when assessment is conceptualized as a pedagogical decision-making process, teachers and students use evidence to keep learning developing continuously. Teachers are able to make contingent evidence-based pedagogical responses, such as the practices of scaffolding described in chapter 2, which are intended to advance learning.[8]

In many other countries, for example, Australia, New Zealand, the United Kingdom, and Canada, assessment at the heart of pedagogy has been characterized as assessment *for* learning.[9] This term stands in contrast to the formulation assessment *of* learning, which denotes the summative function of assessment. In the United States, the term "formative assessment" is more widely adopted, although along with this adoption comes a range of different notions of what it means. For example, in the United States, formative assessment is often referred to as a measurement event, as in the formulation "assessment for formative purposes." When framed as assessment for formative purposes, the assessment becomes an instrument designed to check the attainment of a set of predetermined objectives in order to either fix failings or target the next level of objectives.[10]

The perspective we take here is of formative assessment as assessment *for* learning, reflecting that it is a process, not a measurement instrument *per se*, that is integrated into ongoing teaching and learning for all students, and as we will see, especially for ELLs, who are learning language, content, and analytical practices simultaneously. When enacted as a pedagogical process, formative assessment has a beneficial effect on learning and achievement.[11]

What Is Formative Assessment?

In their landmark review of studies related to formative assessment, Paul Black and Dylan Wiliam define formative assessment as "the process used by teachers to recognize and respond to student learning, in order to enhance that learning, during the learning."[12] This definition locates formative assessment as a process that is integral to teaching and learning.

In addition, Black and Wiliam identify elements of the process, including sharing learning goals and success criteria with students, developing classroom talk as a source of evidence, using evidence to make pedagogical responses, giving feedback to move learning forward, activating students as resources for their own learning through self-assessment, and activating students as resources for one another through peer assessment.[13] All of these elements are particularly relevant for ELLs, since they support the kinds of pedagogical shifts that allow for a rich learning environment where learning content, analytical practices, and language can take place simultaneously.

In the next section, we will take a look at each of the elements of the formative assessment process and consider how they support ELL students and their teachers to advance both language and content learning.

SHARING LEARNING GOALS AND SUCCESS CRITERIA

Learning goals indicate what students are going to learn during a lesson— one or more class periods. They do not represent what students are going to do. What students do is the content of the lesson, which is designed to assist students in meeting the learning goal. Learning goals for ELLs center on content and language learning, ways of engaging in academic practices, communicating, and being able to use language for different purposes and audiences. For example, a third-grade class working toward the ELA standard, "Distinguish their own point of view from that of the narrator or those of the characters," might formulate a lesson learning goal as, "Today, we are going to learn about clues we can use to find out a character's point of view."

Success criteria specify what counts as evidence of learning. They are aligned to the learning goal and indicate what students need to say, do, or write to show that they have met the goal. Learning goals and success criteria also need to be conveyed to students in ways that make them clear, and so that students understand what is expected of them and can monitor their own progress. For the goal described above, success criteria could be (1) write words and phrases the author uses to show the character's point of view; (2) explain to a partner why you think these words and phrases show point of view; (3) choose a line in the text that you think conveys the character's point of view, and say what you think the point of view is.

It should be noted that learning goals and success criteria are not narrow prescriptions of curriculum objectives. Elliot Eisner suggests a useful way to think about them: "The criteria to be met are specified, but the form the solution is to take is not."[14] This perspective is particularly important in regard to language learning. Students do not learn language by accurately repeating target language structures reflective of the audio-lingual approach, or by learning grammar drills that characterized peda-gogy informed by early formal theories, discussed in chapter 3. Instead, guided by their teachers in the context of rich classroom talk with others, they develop their own expertise in language use for particular purposes. Of course, formulaic expressions may be given to students to assist them in acquiring expertise, but students use these as a tool to expand their language rather than a prescription of how they should speak or write. To illustrate, let us explore an example from a fourth-grade dual-language program class composed of both ELLs and English-only students.[15]

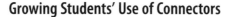

Growing Students' Use of Connectors

I n ELA, Ms. Viera's fourth-grade students were learning about making claims and providing evidence in argument structures. Listening to the students' discussions about text they had read, Ms. Viera recognized that all of her students had a limited repertoire of connectors. Most students, including her ELLs, used the connectors *and*, *then*, and *so* almost exclu-sively. Based on this observation, she decided to focus on expanding stu-dents' repertoires of connectors to more precisely express their ideas and the relationships between them (an analytical practice). She created a chart, shown in figure 4.1, that she used as a teaching tool, and made it available to students as a guide to support their use of connectors.

Using the chart as an illustration, Ms. Viera discussed the goal of increasing the student repertoire of connectors, and identified the success

FIGURE 4.1   Classroom chart to support use of connectors

Making claims and providing evidence
Beginning

First, _____.

One reason is _____.

On one hand, _____.

Middle

Next, _____.

Another example is _____.

In fact, _____.

In the same way, _____.

Equally important is _____.

For instance, _____.

Specifically, _____.

End

Lastly, _____.

In other words, _____.

Above all, _____.

Most important, _____.

Furthermore, _____.

Consequently, _____.

In summary, _____.

criterion as, "When you are talking or writing about claims and evidence, we will notice that you are using some of these connectors, or others that you learn about, to express your ideas more clearly and connect them together better." As a result of her explanation, students were clear about the ELA goal, the language goal, and the success criterion, which meant they could monitor their own learning as well as provide feedback to peers.

Ms. Viera provided a range of opportunities for her students to listen to the various connectors she used in her own speech, and she drew attention to them as they read argument text together. She and her students talked about how various connectors connected ideas in important relationships so that the meaning of what they were hearing or reading was clarified. Eventually, she began to hear the students attempt to use the connectors during their discussions. She provided feedback to the students, giving hints about how they could use the connectors to link ideas more effectively within argument structure. She also used her observations to provide minilessons in which the students examined the function of certain connectors in expressing relationships. The students noticed when their peers used connectors and provided feedback about the effects of the connector on the clarity of the idea they were expressing. Then, after a period of rehearsing the use of connectors orally, without prompting from the teacher, the students began to use a range of connectors in their writing.

Sometimes the ELL students in the class used the connectors in ways that were not entirely accurate. However, consistent with some of the pedagogical ideas presented in chapters 1 and 2, Ms. Viera did not correct their usage. Instead, she validated the students' efforts—they were, after all, beginning to expand their use of connectors—maintaining their legitimacy in accomplishing the work of communication. She would use her observations at a later stage and find opportunities to clarify the use of the inaccurate connectors in ways that preserved the students' confidence and continued willingness to engage in oral and written discourse.

Ms. Viera did not set narrow objectives for her students. Instead, she focused their attention on a range of connectors and gave them opportunities to hear and read them in context. She did not prescribe how they would be used to show relationships and clarify ideas. That was left solely within the students' purview.

CLASSROOM TALK AS A SOURCE OF EVIDENCE

If teachers want to know how well students are using language and understanding content, a primary way is through classroom talk. In all the vignettes we have presented, teachers generated opportunities for classroom talk as a means for their students to develop content knowledge, analytical practices, and language use. They also have used classroom talk as a source of evidence for guiding pedagogical decisions in order to respond to the needs of students as these needs emerged.

Rich classroom talk does not just happen. It has to be carefully planned and engineered. As a prerequisite for classroom talk, teachers need to establish expected routines and participant structures that enable students to engage with the teacher or peers in joint activity.[16] Creating a culture of respect for others' ideas and for the language that is used to express them is also an important prerequisite for classroom talk. No student, particularly an ELL student, is going to be willing to speak English if she fears ridicule or criticism from her teacher or peers. Students need to be taught the classroom norms of how to listen carefully to each other, build on each other's ideas, present alternative viewpoints, and provide feedback in constructive ways. These norms were evident in Ms. Cardenas's classroom, described in chapter 1. We saw the students engaging in productive discussions with each other, comparing their research findings about the desert cactuses and routinely offering feedback to peers in support of learning. These student practices of interaction and behavior were the result of careful cultivation by the teacher, and were strengthened through a process of continual monitoring.

With these prerequisites in place, teachers have created the conditions in which their students can be provided with opportunities to participate in substantive discussions that not only offer a source of evidence for teachers, but also support students' individual and collective learning.

Similarly in chapter 2, newcomers to the United States engaged in substantive conversations that had been stimulated by the teacher. The students had observed a simulation about atoms and were then prompted by the teacher to come up with questions about what they had just seen. In their interactions, we saw students engaged in formulating questions, using whatever English they had acquired to that point to communicate with each other. Notably, the students were listening for the meaning that their peers were conveying and were supporting each other in their communicative process. As students discussed their questions in pairs, the teacher was able to obtain evidence of how the students were using language to express their science knowledge and to raise questions. In essence, she was able to assess language use, analytical practices, and content knowledge together.

Another way to engineer classroom talk is to ask questions of students to encourage extended discourse, a valuable source of evidence about students' language use and content understanding. However, forms of questioning lodged in the initiation-response-evaluation (IRE) model will not give students opportunities to engage in extended discourse.[17] In the IRE model, teachers ask a question, students respond to the question with what they believe is the correct answer, and then teachers provide an evaluation as to whether the answer is correct or not, moving on to other students in the event that the answer is incorrect. This practice represents a traditional, and perhaps prevailing, form of questioning in American schools.[18] It is a practice that neither helps students to explore important ideas and relationships, nor permits teachers to gain insights into student thinking and the extent of their language use. Tony Edwards has referred to this kind of classroom talk as embodying "unequal communicative rights for those who 'know' and those who do not."[19] If classroom talk is to make a meaningful contribution to the development of students' language learning and thinking, "it must move beyond the acting out of such cognitively restricting rituals."[20]

In the following example, we provide an illustration of equal communicative rights, and we see how questioning can initiate productive discourse to provide a source of evidence of mathematical understanding and disciplinary language use.

Questioning Elicits Students' Building of Content Knowledge and Language Skills

In this lesson, third-grade ELL students are working on applying their knowledge of addition and multiplication to solving problems. The problem they have been asked to solve is as follows: "Ricardo had 135 U.S. stamps. He had three times as many foreign stamps. How many stamps did he have altogether?" The teacher, Ms. Castenada, preconstructs the task in terms of "three steps" to solve the problem in the following sequence, which eventuates in the class stating that they need to identify (1) the question, (2) the clues, and (3) keywords.

> **Ms. Castenada:** I want you to discuss what we need to know in order to solve this problem. And there are three steps. Who can remember one of the three steps to solve this problem? Daniel?
>
> **Daniel:** Identify a question.
>
> **Ms. Castenada:** Okay. Then we identify a question.
>
> **Alex:** We identify the clues.
>
> **Ms. Castenada:** Okay. Then we identify the clues. Go ahead, Alejandra.
>
> **Alejandra:** Look for keywords.
>
> **Ms. Castenada:** And keywords. I want you all to turn to your partner, and I want you to identify all three. The questions, the clues—remember, there might be more than just one—and the keywords. Now go ahead and discuss that together.

While the students are discussing the problem in twos and threes, Ms. Castenada moves among the groups and explores their progress. She joins Ricardo, Danny, and Carlos and listens in for a brief time before she asks them:

> **Ms. Castenada:** Can anyone inform me of what you are working on? Can you tell me a little bit more about what you are doing as a group?
>
> **Ricardo:** Well, we're trying to find out if it's multiplication or division. We kind of thinks its multiplication 'cuz you could tell here . . . well, first we highlighted the clue, and then we shaped all the clues because it says "Ricardo had 135 U.S. stamps," and then we read the next sentence: "He has three times as many foreign stamps" as U.S. stamps. So then, right when it says has three times as many, we might think that's multiplication. 'Cuz

you know how in division, it says "in each," mostly in division it says "in each" and mostly in multiplication it says "times."

Ms. Castenada: So, the word "times" is already a clue informing you that this problem could be a multiplication problem [student nods]. So you're using clues. Now, what is the question—what it is that they want you to solve?

Danny: They are asking us to solve how many do we have altogether. Like all of 'em ... three times as many as 135 ... and that would be like adding 135, 135, 135. But since we're working on multiplication and division, we have to do it the opposite way. It means dividing to find out the answer ... to get three times as many as 135.

Ms. Castenada: Danny, when you were reading the question—and I am going to have you read it one more time, and I want to ask the rest of us to just listen while he's reading the question. I want you to really notice what he is saying and see if we can find any other keywords within that question. OK, go ahead, Danny. [Danny reads the question again.] Mmmm—so how many stamps did he have altogether? [Ricardo raises his hand.] Ricardo?

Ricardo: Well there's actually two of 'em—and there's altogether and one other, how much does it equal and how many.

Ms. Castenada: So the word "altogether" informs you of what?

Ricardo: They wanna ..., they're asking us, how much does it equal?

Danny: How much does it all [waves his hand in sweeping motion].

Ms. Castenada: Well, it started off as multiplication when listening to you, and you felt that this was really a multiplication problem when looking at the word times. But when Danny reread the question, it seemed that it was an addition problem.

Carlos: And a multiplication problem.

Ms. Castenada: Do you think it might be both?

Carlos: Yeah.

Danny: You could probably put 'em both together and solve.

Ms. Castenada: Do you think that's what they're asking you to do? Are those the next steps? So maybe multiplication and addition? I'm going to leave that one up to you. See what you come up with.

Ricardo: Sometimes multiplication could be close to division [*sic*]. Sometimes you don't always have to multiply. You could just like keep on adding, keep on adding. So three times. So you could do 1, 135, 1, 135, 1, 135, and then you'll find the sum.

Ms. Castenada: Does anyone know what we call that, when we add a number over and over and over?

Danny: Repeashis. [Danny attempts to say *repeated*.]

Ms. Castenada: Pretty close. It's called repeated addition. Do you remember the term "repeated addition"? [Both students nod.]

Danny: I have an idea. [Ms. C: Yes?] Why don't we . . . first we do the problem there's multiplication. Then the next problem . . . we do it again, but this time addition. And the last one, we could do it as division . . . So if we has it all the same, we have the answer.

Ms. Castenada: Well, I'm going to leave that up to you as a group . . . and I want you to really think . . . what would be your next step, and determine if you would use those three steps. Would you start with multiplication and then add? And if that's the case, what would you be multiplying and what would you be adding? OK? [Students nod.] Okay, go ahead and continue.

———————— ◆ ————————

Ms. Castenada's interaction is designed to elicit student thinking about the problem and to invite the students to use mathematical language to explain their ideas. After her original question, "Can you tell me a little bit more about what you are doing as a group?" it is noticeable that Ms. Castenada does not ask very many questions, and that most of those she does ask are framed so as to invite ideas rather than to prescribe modes of thinking or communication. In fact, most of her contributions are conversational, reflecting what the students have conjectured while simultaneously nudging their thinking to connect multiplication and addition as components of the problem's solution.

In the course of these exchanges, Ms. Castenada has obtained important evidence about the students' understanding of the relationship between multiplication and addition: they have an emergent grasp of the connection between the two. She has also learned that they are much less clear about the relationship between multiplication and division. Finally, she has determined that the students can use the steps she identified at the outset of the lesson to help them understand what solving the problem entails.

At no point in the interaction does Ms. Castenada overtly correct any student's inaccurate language or prescribe a course of action. She leaves apparent errors of mathematical reasoning on the table, trusting that the students' further thinking will clarify the issue, and knowing that she will have other opportunities to address persisting difficulties in subsequent rounds of conversation.

It is striking that these students entered kindergarten speaking no English, yet in their fourth year of school, they are able to engage in extended mathematical discourse using precise mathematical language, even though their English grammar is inaccurate from time to time. From their discussion of the question's clues, to the relationship between addition and multiplication, the students are using English to make meaning of the problem, develop analytical practices, and communicate their ideas about its solution. The enabling context of Ms. Castenada's questions undoubtedly contributes to this outcome.

GIVING FEEDBACK TO MOVE LEARNING FORWARD

Giving feedback to students while their learning is developing has a powerful influence on that learning.[21] However, not all types of feedback are effective. Feedback that is critical, that is comparative and indicates a student's standing relative to peers, that is vague and lacks specificity, or that draws attention to the student rather than the task can have negative effects on learning.[22] Feedback is effective when it is related to learning goals and success criteria; when it is specific and clear; when it provides suggestions, hints, or cues rather than correct answers; and when it involves students cognitively in the task.[23] This kind of feedback informs and leads thinking forward.[24]

In the vignette below, we see a teacher who is engaged in a conversation with one of her ELL students and whose feedback to the student reflects all the characteristics of effective feedback.

---------◆---------

Interactional Feedback Serves Student Agency

In Ms. Lozano's fifth-grade writing class, the students are learning about argument structure. So far, the students have learned about arguments and counterarguments, and now they are incorporating these structures into their own writing. Angie is involved in independent writing when Ms. Lozano comes to sit beside her and they have the following conversation:

Ms. Lozano: Okay, Angie, what are you working on?

Angie: I'm working on my final draft, and wanted to make it kind of sentences, and I wanted your feedback.

Ms. Lozano: Okay. Do we have our success criteria here?

Angie: Yes [Angie points to the paper on which the criteria are written].

Ms. Lozano: What are you looking at right now, what are you focusing on? Are you focusing on punctuation? Are you focusing on grammar?

Angie: I'm working on this one [pointing to her criteria].

Ms. Lozano: Oh, clarity, so you're asking yourself if this is going to make sense to somebody who has no idea. So what do you think so far?

Angie: I don't know if I should . . . because I started with two questions and then I ended with a period. And then I started another question.

Ms. Lozano: I see, so let's read it and see how that makes sense.

Angie: It says "The world has been taken by trash . . . What are you going to do to save our earth?" [Angie continues to read her writing.]

Ms. Lozano: Okay, let's go back to your original concern. So, you're concerned about having two questions at the beginning. Well, the question that you have here at the beginning, "I wonder why people don't pick up trash?" Well, following that up with what, what is this? "People may argue that," what is that?

Angie: That's a counterargument.

Ms. Lozano: That's a counterargument. So this question, "I wonder why people don't pick up trash?"

Angie: Is connected to my counterargument.

Ms. Lozano: Is connected to your counterargument. So it makes sense. Okay? So what's the other question that you feel maybe . . .

Angie: I was going to put, right here, after "about 33 billion people don't care about the earth," I was going to put "I wonder why they don't care?" And then I was going to put this one [points to the next line in her writing].

Ms. Lozano: Oh, I see.

Angie: And I wanted to know if that was okay. To put two questions in a question, period, and another question.

Ms. Lozano: Well, I think that "I wonder why they don't care" and "I wonder why people don't pick up trash"—it's connected. It's connected. So is there a way that you think maybe you can combine those two into one? So that you don't have two questions back to back?

Angie: Yeah.

Ms. Lozano: So can you think about that? Because "I wonder why they don't care" and "I wonder why people don't pick up trash" . . .

Angie: Are the same.

> **Ms. Lozano:** Are connected to each other. So you can definitely think about connecting those two so that it's one question. But that has those two things, those two components, that you wanted to make sure were in there.
>
> **Angie:** Okay.
>
> **Ms. Lozano:** So go ahead and think about how you can do that.

◆

Angie is soliciting assistance in her writing, and she does so in response to Ms. Lozano's question, "What are you working on?" In going beyond the agenda of Ms. Lozano's question, Angie clearly takes the initiative in requesting feedback about her work. Angie has already written a rhetorical question, "I wonder why people don't pick up the trash?" and she is entertaining the idea of a second question back to back, "I wonder why people don't care [about the earth]?" Ms. Lozano checks her understanding of Angie's problem, "So, you are concerned . . . ," and by looking at Angie's text finds that her rhetorical question is immediately followed by text that is clearly identifiable as the beginnings of a counterargument. Having arrived at this point, Ms. Lozano is ready to engage Angie's question about writing two questions consecutively, a concern that Angie specifically renews when she says, "And I wanted to know if that was okay. To put two questions in a question, period, and another question."

Without addressing this question directly, Ms. Lozano observes that the two questions are closely connected, and asks if Angie can think of a way of combining "those two into one." Across this entire sequence, Ms. Lozano sustains an interactional stance in which her job is to come to an understanding of the problem with which Angie is presently grappling. While not providing a correct answer, Ms. Lozano's feedback offers Angie a way out of her dilemma: combine the two questions into one "so that you don't have two questions back to back." Subsequently, she invites Angie to "go ahead and think about how you can do that."

In this sequence, Ms. Lozano engaged in a series of contingent questions and responses, mostly propelled by Angie's concerns, and engaged her cognitively in the task. She provided targeted and suggestive feedback to Angie's concerns, maintaining the student's role as an active agent in her learning who could construct the way forward herself.

Additionally, during the course of the exchange, Ms. Lozano obtained evidence of Angie's understanding of argument structure. She was also able to listen to English language capabilities in expressing her understanding, notably not correcting grammatical errors, such as "wanted to make it kind of sentences," and incomplete statements, such as "To put two questions in a question, period, and another question." Angie was clearly, if not always accurately, conveying her concern, and the purpose of this interaction was to address her concern through feedback.

There is a startling contrast between Ms. Lozano's response to Angie and the response that we saw in chapter 3 from May's teacher to May's essay about her family's harrowing experience when they escaped from their home village in her war-torn country. May's essay, which clearly communicated her powerful personal experience, had prompted the feedback, "You have had an exciting life! Please watch verbs in the past tense." Not only does this feedback diminish May's experience and her efforts to communicate it in writing, it does not assist May in her learning. If May knew how to conjugate verbs in the past tense, she would very likely have done so. Simply telling May to "watch" those verbs does not provide her with any insights about verbs in the past tense that she might be able to use in her oral and written language. A response aimed at helping her to understand that she was overgeneralizing the rule for the past tense in English to verbs that do not follow that pattern would have been useful feedback that she would have been able to use in revising her work or in future work.

INVOLVING STUDENTS THROUGH SELF-ASSESSMENT AND PEER ASSESSMENT

Learning is the property of students, since no one else can learn for them.
While teachers can regulate opportunities for student learning, only the student can actually regulate his or her learning.[25] Self-assessment is an essential process for self-regulation, as it entails students' becoming

aware of the goals of their learning and the criteria for meeting those goals, monitoring progress toward reaching those goals, and taking action when they determine they are not making the desired progress.[26]

Self-assessment differs from self-evaluation or self-rating (often done with the use of rubrics), which generally involve assigning a score or grade.[27] Instead, self-assessment occurs during the learning process; it functions as a learning strategy through which students monitor their progress during the execution of a task and modify their actions based on their determination of how well they are meeting established criteria.[28]

When students are actively monitoring their progress to meet their goal, they adopt a stance of greater agency toward their own learning. We saw this agentive stance clearly in the interaction between Angie and Ms. Lozano. In the process of monitoring her writing against the established criteria related to "clarity," Angie requested feedback from her teacher and initiated the topic in her conversation with her. Angie was not involved in self-rating—giving herself a score against a rubric—but rather was monitoring her writing as she was doing it.

Students need to learn how to engage in self-assessment. As a first step in self-assessment, students must understand the purpose of assessment more broadly. In a study of a nationally representative sample of students' perceptions of classroom assessment, the majority of students reported that the purpose of assessment was to give them a grade or a score.[29] These students did not understand, nor had likely experienced, that the purpose of assessment is to provide feedback to them and their teachers. In such circumstances, it may be hard to convince students of the value of self-assessment. However, it is important that students are aware of the value of self-assessment and understand that it is a crucial ability for learning.

Students can learn to self-assess through a number of strategies: (1) by using established criteria that help them visualize quality, with support from their teacher about how to use them; (2) by observing models (such as teacher think-alouds) and then expressing their own think-alouds with feedback from the teacher; (3) through continued practice in doing a learning task and engaging with teachers and peers for their opinions about how well they are self-assessing and how they might improve; (4) by being provided with structures; and (5) by having opportunities to return to learning tasks so that improvements can be made based on their self-assessment.[30] Taken together, these strategies promote students' capabilities in self-assessment, permitting them to be active agents in their own learning.

Returning to Ms. Cardenas's classroom from chapter 1, we see that she is assisting students to become skilled in self-assessment. In prior lessons, she has taught the students to read "with the [research] question in mind." In their cactus study, the students are reading a variety of sources to help answer their research questions. To assist their self-assessment process as they read, Ms. Cardenas has provided them with the structure of several questions:

> Does this fact from the text help answer my question?
> What about this fact helps answer my question?
> How do I know?
> What words and sentences in the text help me think that?

When she involves students in discussion about their research, she refers to these questions, supporting them in self-assessment and also ascribing value to the process. As she discusses the findings with the students, she is not only using self-assessment to contribute to the students' learning and their development of self-regulation, she is also gaining insights into both how they are processing written language and how well they are using language to express their ideas.

Another example of supporting students in self-assessment is found in chapter 3 in the six clarifying bookmark strategies, which students can employ when they encounter text that is beyond their reach. In a process of self-assessment and self-regulation, students monitor their own reading, make decisions about when they need to modify their reading approach because the text is problematic, and determine the most effective strategy for clarifying their understanding of the text. The students remain in control of their learning via the support structure provided them.

In addition to self-assessment, another role for students in formative assessment is to act as resources for each other through peer assessment and feedback. Just as self-assessment does not mean that students self-grade or self-rate, formative peer assessment does not mean that students rate or grade each other's work so that the teacher doesn't have to—that is summative peer assessment. Formative peer assessment entails students reviewing each other's work against established criteria and making suggestions for improvement.[31] When students are activated as resources for each other in this way, the responsibility for learning does not reside solely with the teacher or individual students, but is distributed across the entire class.

In Ms. Cardenas's classroom in chapter 1, students engaged in peer assessment as they collected the information relevant to their question. For example, pairs discussed their findings and provided each other with feedback based on their assessment, such as, "I suggest that you highlight everywhere information was gathered so you know what sources to cite. This will also help keep you organized."

Skills in peer assessment also need to be taught. Just as with self-assessment, students need to be aware of the importance of peer assessment and the contribution it can make to learning. Many of the same strategies that support self-assessment can be used to help students develop skills in peer assessment. Teacher models of assessment and feedback are primary ways to enculturate students in peer assessment. Making assessment criteria explicit is another. For example, Ms. Cardenas made clear to her students the criteria for a successful oral presentation and successful audience behavior during and after the presentation as a guide for the students' performance and for peer assessment. In the case of ELLs in particular, formulaic expressions, which promote the appropriation of the language students can use, are valuable for peer assessment. For example, sentence beginnings such as "Could you clarify what you mean when you say . . ." and "Perhaps you could think about . . ." provide a structure from which students can develop their responses to other students in a peer-feedback context.

Peer assessment is beneficial to the person providing the feedback as well as to the students who are receiving feedback. These benefits are well captured by Dylan Wiliam:

> . . . because in thinking through what it is that this piece of work represents and what needs to happen to improve it, the students are forced to internalize success criteria and they're able to do it in the context of someone else's work, which is less emotionally charged than your own.

So what we routinely see . . . we see very, very commonly is when students have given feedback to others about a piece of work, their own subsequent attempts at that same work are much improved because they're now much clearer about what good work in that task looks like.[32]

Taken together, all of the practices discussed above—establishing goals and success criteria, obtaining and acting upon evidence, and involving students in self-assessment and peer assessment—characterize the successful implementation of formative assessment for ELLs. However, none of these practices can be effective if the classroom context is not conducive to their enactment.

Classroom Context

In chapter 3 we introduced the idea of legitimacy for language learners. Legitimacy for ELLs is realized when their teachers and peers create the circumstances in which they have the opportunities to become competent language speakers. ELLs' emerging English, although linguistically imperfect, must be supported and nurtured by the classroom community so that each student can gradually become a competent language user, regardless of his or her starting point. Legitimacy is a prerequisite for formative assessment.

A classroom context for legitimacy is, first and foremost, the result of teachers' beliefs and attitudes. Teachers who believe that ELLs can learn subject matter content while acquiring English are much more likely to establish high expectations for their ELL students than those who do not. And we know the value of high expectations—students will rise to meet them. When high expectations, combined with appropriate support, are clearly in place, students understand that their teachers believe they can achieve them. When they are not, students equally understand that their teachers do not think they are capable of reaching high standards. In these circumstances, it is not difficult to imagine a lack of motivation on the students' part.

Legitimacy is also maintained when students interact with each other within the participant structures the teacher has established and use language for particular purposes in order to develop their linguistic competence. In each of the classroom examples discussed in this chapter, we saw students participating in purposeful language activity with their teacher and with each other. Language activities enabled by the participant structures also become occasions for formative assessment when both teachers and students can attend to language use in the content areas and determine what students need to learn next.

Finally, legitimacy requires that the relationships in the classroom are learning focused. This means that relationships among peers and between students and teachers are squarely centered on learning. More specifically, a relationship between a teacher and his or her students is learning focused when the teacher's sole purpose is to support learning to meet high expectations. The student's role in the relationship is simply to learn, focusing on the question "what needs to happen in this lesson to help me learn, and what do I need to do?"[33] Similarly, the relationships between and among students center on what students can do to support each other's learning. In this context, student agency can flourish, because each student is responsible for his or her own and for each other's learning.

When relationships are learning focused, ELLs can feel assured that their emerging and approximate English will not be subject to overt correction or sanction. Teachers will also be able to obtain the evidence they need about students' language and content learning to understand what they need to do day-by-day to support students' continued progress and achieve the aspirations of the new standards.

CHAPTER 5

◆

The Role of Summative Assessment

Key Leverage Points and Stress Points in Assessing ELLs

E nglish language learner (ELL) group status, unlike that of any other
student group, is meant to be temporary. Federal and state policies
anticipate that ELLs will leave this category as a result of language instruction and academic support services that they are entitled to receive by
law. Decisions about whether and when students enter, advance through,
and exit the ELL subgroup are made based on assessment results. Such
assessments are distinct from the formative assessment practices that we
discussed in the previous chapter. Formative assessment rests squarely
within a teacher's classroom practice and is clearly intended to support
contingent pedagogy day-by-day while students are developing their language use and engaging in deep and transferable content learning. Yet
these formative assessment practices take place within a wider assessment
context encompassing assessments *of* learning that are often mandated
by federal, state, or district policies. Such assessments serve a summative purpose, and because they "sum up" what learning students have
achieved after a period of time, they are sometimes referred to as assessments *of* learning. Their use has significant implications for ELLs and
their teachers.

In this chapter, we focus on assessments of learning that ELLs encounter during their educational experience. We cast a wide net in order to capture a broad overview of the assessment landscape and to highlight some key leverage points and stress points in ELL assessment. We begin by considering how ELLs are defined.

Defining ELLs

The concept of an English language learner is in part a policy and legal construct. For example, in the federal Elementary and Secondary Education Act (ESEA), ELLs are defined as students from an environment where a language other than, or in addition to, English is spoken, and "whose difficulties in speaking, reading, writing, or understanding the English language may be sufficient to deny [them] the ability to meet the State's proficient level of achievement on State assessments; the ability to successfully achieve in classrooms where the language of instruction is English; or the opportunity to participate fully in society."[1] This definition of a "limited English proficient" student derives from federal civil rights and case law that establishes ELLs as a federally protected class of students.[2] However, inherent in this definition is an orientation toward ELLs of language deficiency. As we saw in chapter 1, ELLs are a diverse group, and come to school from differing backgrounds and language groups. In its deficit orientation, the federal definition, and the many statutes and legal decisions underlying it, do not acknowledge what ELL students *can do* with their home language or English, or how their home language might be leveraged to assist in learning an additional language. Instead, the orientation and language of much legislation and case law suggest ELLs are "limited English proficient" and foreclosed from any meaningful educational opportunity without English; they require language "remediation" to overcome English language "deficits," and are at risk of incurring "irreparable academic deficits" while doing so.[3]

Of course, these laws were passed and upheld in the 1960s, 1970s, and early 1980s in response to a systematic neglect of ELL students' educational rights. Yet such problematic conceptualizations have their own suggestive power and exist in tension with newer understandings from a range of behavioral sciences. Throughout the preceding chapter, we have stressed these new understandings about how students learn, and how language, content knowledge, and analytical practices can develop simultaneously.

Beyond federal case law and legislation defining ELLs, states also have definitions of what constitutes ELL status. There is variation among these definitions, and they are operationalized differently across states, often even varying within a state. This definitional disparity was studied in a 2011 National Research Council report, which concluded that widespread variations in the English language proficiency and academic standards, assessments, and performance criteria used to determine ELL status have led to inconsistent and noncomparable definitions of an ELL.[4] Spurred by federal requirements of the two Race to the Top academic consortia and the two English language proficiency (ELP) assessment consortia, and supported by the Council of Chief State School Officers, a multi-state effort involving state and local educators, researchers, professional associations, advocacy groups, and other stakeholders has explored ways to move toward more common conceptions, criteria, and practices to define ELLs more consistently within and across states.[5] These efforts are described later in the chapter.

Thus, at present, millions of students across the United States receive the ELL designation based on assessment practices, tools, and outcomes. In the next section we discuss the practices and assessments that are used for the purpose of determining ELL status.

Assessment Use to Determine ELL Status

In most states, home language surveys completed by parents or guardians at initial school registration are used to determine if a student uses or understands a language other than or in addition to English. If so, the student is considered a potential ELL and is given an initial assessment of English language proficiency to confirm (or disconfirm) his or her ELL status. Most states and local school districts use ELP as well as academic performance standards to determine an ELL's progress and readiness for exit. This means that assessment results on ELP tests and academic achievement tests, given in English, are central in determining exit from ELL status. But using academic achievement tests for this purpose is problematic, and we discuss this issue further below.

As has long been noted, any assessment given *in* English—no matter the academic subject matter—will for ELLs also be an assessment *of* English, at least to some extent.[6] For this reason, ELLs' level of language proficiency substantially influences their academic test performance. Recent research has explored the relationship between ELLs' assessed English language proficiency and their performance on academic content assessments. Using data for ELA and mathematics from one state at grade 4, we illustrate the common pattern of this relationship for ELL students in figure 5.1.[7]

Figure 5.1 displays boxplots showing the distribution of ELLs' scale scores on a state's ELA (top graph) and mathematics assessments (bottom graph) on the y axes, in relation to their assessed state ELP test levels (1 through 5) on the x axes. The horizontal line extending from the y axis of each graph identifies the "proficient" performance standard on the state's academic content assessments. In the boxplots, the diamond inside each box is the mean score, and the line in the center of the box is the median score. The top and bottom of each box show where the top 25 percent and bottom 25 percent, respectively, of ELLs at that ELP level perform on the academic content assessment.

First, these data show a general pattern. Students' academic performance increases as their ELP level increases. ELLs at the lowest ELP levels (levels 1 and 2) perform in a much lower assessed range than ELLs at higher ELP levels. Second, the overall performance of ELLs is higher on math than on ELA at each ELP level. For example, just over half of ELLs at ELP level 3 ("intermediate") on this test score proficient on the math assessment, while less than 25 percent do so in ELA.[8] For ELLs at ELP level 4 ("early advanced"), over 50 percent score proficient on the ELA assessment, while 75 percent do so in mathematics.[9] Finally, although the pattern of increased academic performance with increased ELP level holds, there is still overlap in academic performance by students across adjacent ELP levels in both subject areas. Although the ELP level labels of different ELP tests vary, similar patterns of performance are seen consistently across different tests, grade levels, and states in other analyses.[10]

FIGURE 5.1   ELL English language arts and mathematics performance by ELP level

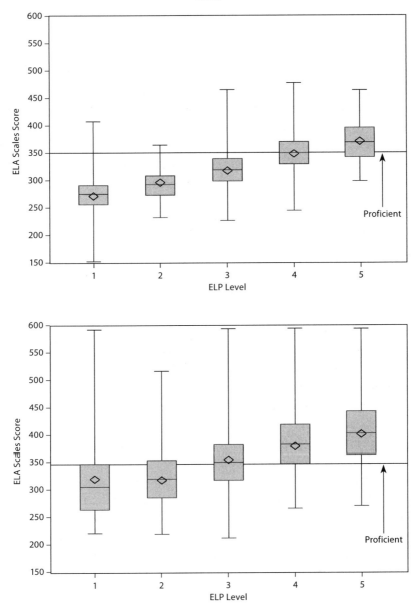

What we learn from this analysis is that ELL students' academic test performance varies systematically by their level of English language proficiency. This relationship is stronger for subjects like ELA, which are ostensibly more language intensive compared to math. Yet, while language is a key factor, the overlapping ranges of performance across ELP levels suggest that other factors also influence these outcomes. For example, ELLs at adjacent ELP levels may be afforded different opportunities to engage with disciplinary concepts and analytical practices through well-designed curriculum and well-scaffolded pedagogy. Also, students may differ substantially in their amount of time in the system, prior formal schooling experience, level of primary language literacy, or other linguistic or academic resources in their environments, as we saw in the vignettes in previous chapters.

What might teachers take away from such commonly seen patterns of performance? Clearly, the way in which the assessments are currently constructed and used leads to the conclusion that students' developing language proficiency is related to their ability to demonstrate knowledge and skills on content assessments using English. As we maintain throughout the book, ELL students' conceptual understandings, analytical practices, and dynamic language uses are inseparably intertwined and can be developed simultaneously. Yet the overlaps in student performance across ELP levels also suggest that ELLs' English language proficiency is not the sole determinant of their academic performance. At some point (in these data, the "early advanced" level) it largely ceases to be a predictor of academic performance.

Extending this "take away" from these patterns of performance, teachers and site administrators should also beware of poorly aligned assessments, as well as of conceptions of language development and uncoordinated assessment policies that promote sequential and dichotomous views of language and content development. In particular, viewing ELLs' language proficiency as a prerequisite for engaging with rigorous grade-level content and assessing these dimensions using unrelated standards can lead to separate, inequitable curricular tracks, an artificial division of labor among educators, and faulty decisions.[11] For example, ESL teachers and the ESL instructional period might wrongly be viewed as who develops students' language uses and when, and disconnect both from the academic curriculum. Also, ELLs may be excluded from more rigorous content-learning opportunities that are deemed inaccessible, and receive remedial or "sheltered" instruction using simplified materials and language (that are often intellectually less rigorous as well). Indeed, some ELL students may exhibit lower academic achievement for reasons that have little or nothing to do with their English language proficiency, but rather are a result of the lack of rigorous curriculum and learning opportunities they receive. As we saw in previous chapters, with effective pedagogy, ELLs across a range of English language proficiency can engage in demanding content learning, which in turn further develops their academic uses of language.

At least annually, ELL status is assessed and decisions are made to exit students from this subgroup using results from ELP tests and often from academic achievement assessments. When students meet the required performance criteria, they exit ELL status. While some students leave the ELL cohort, other students remain and newly arrived students enter based on their assessment results. We characterize this reality as a revolving door, and next describe a number of problems associated with it.

EXITING ELL STATUS AND THE REVOLVING DOOR PHENOMENON

The first problem with the revolving door of continuously exiting and entering ELLs is one of reporting. Two years after students have exited ELL status, their academic achievement outcomes are no longer counted in the ELL subgroup. Those not meeting the exit criteria retain the status of ELL and are joined by newly arriving ELLs, who are by definition at lower ELP levels.[12] As a result, ELL subgroup membership is systematically skewed toward lower-performing students. This means that district and state reports on the academic achievement and growth of the "current" ELL subgroup actually underrepresent the students' academic performance and growth. Consequently, the ELL subgroup is portrayed as always underperforming relative to non-ELLs (which include former ELLs!), a situation that ELL students are often acutely aware of and that has the potential to leave them feeling stigmatized.

Second, there is an accountability problem. Underrepresenting ELL performance and growth undermines meaningful accountability for ELLs.[13] Because the current ELL subgroup is by design continually changing, teachers and schools are neither credited nor held accountable for the long-term outcomes of all initial ELL students.[14] For example, initial ELLs at the secondary level who exited the status more than two years earlier are aggregated into the non-ELL group. On a statewide level, these former ELLs generally perform as well as or better than their monolingual English-speaking peers, but this varies greatly from district to district and from school to school.

Educators cannot uncover these variations unless they carefully examine the progress and performance over time of all initial ELLs. Moreover, teachers, administrators, and policy makers will need to always frame any discussion of ELL assessment results by carefully considering which students' results are being referred to, and for what purpose. For example, when examining ELLs' English language arts performance over time on the statewide ELA assessment, educators must "stabilize the cohort." This involves considering all the students that began as ELLs and following their progress over time in order to obtain a complete and accurate picture of their longitudinal performance.[15] So, too, district or state policy makers trying to evaluate high school graduation rates of students entering their systems as ELL, for example, must consider all initial ELL students, which include current and former ELLs. On the other hand, educators aiming to ensure ELL students are progressing and not remaining as ELLs for many years need to disaggregate the performance of current ELLs by their time in the school system and their initial ELP level, or "starting point." This will allow them to more carefully examine progress patterns over time and uncover both strengths and areas needing improvement in instructional services.

As we have seen, assessment practices carry enormous consequences for ELLs. ELL students are assessed in more ways than are non-ELL students. ELP and academic assessment results directly determine who is and who is not in the ELL population. We have also emphasized that, because this group is dynamic and changing over time, it is important that educators carefully analyze ELP and academic assessment results together, and by time in the system, to avoid misinterpreting or misrepresenting students' performance.

While assessment plays a consequential role in determining ELL status, and ongoing formative assessment—or assessment *for* learning—has a critical place in meeting the ongoing needs of ELLs, assessments *of* learning also impact ELL educators' decisions. We now turn to the purposes of these assessments and illustrate the challenges and opportunities ELL teachers and students face in using them.

Assessments of Learning

Assessments of learning generally measure student attainment of intermediate and end-of-year goals. Intermediate goals can range from unit-of-study goals to quarterly learning goals to goals for student learning over the course of a semester. Assessments that address this span of learning are typically referred to as *interim*, or *benchmark*, assessments. Other assessments address longer-term goals, including those for the end of a course of study and for achieving annual grade-level standards, whether these are ELP or academic content standards. Because these assessments cover different periods of learning, they provide information of varying levels of detail and serve different purposes and audiences. We will first consider who uses interim/benchmark assessments and why.

INTERIM/BENCHMARK ASSESSMENTS

District and school leaders increasingly use these forms of assessment. District or school personnel (e.g., subject matter content experts) may develop them, or districts may purchase externally developed assessments for district- or school-wide use. The purpose of these assessments is to measure student achievement in relation to intermediate goals. Educators use the assessment results to inform a number of different actions. When educators examine results with an eye to future actions, they may serve a formative purpose, but as discussed in chapter 4, we make a distinction between assessment use for formative purposes and formative assessment as a pedagogical process designed to inform contingent pedagogy and learning.

The following are among the actions that educators can take based on interim/benchmark results:

- Determine progress between time points;
- Identify students in need of additional support;
- Readjust professional learning priorities and resource decisions;

- Continue or readjust improvement strategies;
- Guide and formatively evaluate curricula and programs;
- Identify promising practices;
- Aggregate results to examine trends in performance, and disaggregate results to examine performance of specific subgroups (e.g., ELLs);
- Report performance to parents;
- Predict outcomes on high-stakes end-of-year assessments.[16]

Clearly, interim/benchmark assessment results are used to inform a wide range of actions, and for this reason, their results may be susceptible to multiple meanings and misunderstandings.[17] Interim/benchmark assessment results are best used by district and school leaders when they clarify the intended primary purpose for the assessment, examine carefully whether the tool appropriately fits that purpose, and guard against multiple purposes that are incompatible or unattainable. Below, we illustrate these points with two uses of interim assessment.

Education leaders often use the results of interim assessments to evaluate the implementation or effectiveness of a particular instructional program or curriculum as a way to gain periodic feedback at a system level about how students are progressing relative to learning expectations. Interim assessments designed for this purpose are usually administered twice a year. Given the infrequency of these assessments, any insights yielded and changes that educators enact will likely occur from year to year, so that students in future years benefit from any improvements. Obvious findings that immediately inform curriculum design or instructional practices can be carried out within the current year, but the assessment's very timing makes this much less likely.

In the instances above, results from interim assessments of learning serve a formative purpose. That is, they provide a starting point for educators to reflect on and discuss students' past performance at a grade, school, or district level. They also signal potential areas to investigate for educational program challenges and for planning professional learning within or across school years. Effective evaluative interim assessments can be designed locally when subject matter experts within a school district (e.g., curriculum specialists, master teachers, instructional coaches) have sufficient content knowledge to design meaningful tasks that capture deeper curriculum goals.[18]

Interim assessments are sometimes designed to predict a student's likely performance on a later (usually high-stakes) annual summative assessment. Although intended to avoid the negative consequences of the latter, using interim assessments for this purpose is very problematic. First, to serve its predictive purpose, the interim assessment must be highly correlated with the annual summative assessment. This means it must test a range of practices beyond what the student has likely been provided sufficient opportunity to learn in the interim time frame, which can lead to identifying as weakness curriculum content that has not yet been introduced. Second, teachers very likely already have a good sense of which students are not progressing toward learning goals. Instead of validly predicting who will fail, they need specific information about what students are not learning, why not, and what to do about it. But the broad curriculum range needed for prediction renders the assessment inadequate for providing the specific information teachers want. In fact, teachers' use of evidence-gathering procedures and tools that reveal which targeted subskills or enabling knowledge a student possesses or not can better serve this purpose.[19] Third, intervening with a student predicted to fail—to the extent that such efforts are successful—undermines the predictive validity of the interim assessment. So the predictive purpose of interim assessments becomes incoherent with any sound theory of learning, and erodes in practice.

While we have consistently emphasized the value of formative assessment practices to ELL students' learning, interim assessments, if used appropriately, can be a valuable source of information for teachers. Results from interim assessments provide periodic snapshots of student learning throughout the year and can serve as a complement to the evidence teachers have obtained and used during the period of learning that the interim assessment addresses. For example, results from interim assessment can help teachers answer these questions:[20]

- What have my students learned so far?
- Who has and who has not met intermediate goals?

- Do the results from these assessments match my judgments of progress from my formative assessment practices?
- What are the strengths and areas of need in my curriculum?
- What are the strengths and areas of need in my instruction?
- What improvements do I need to make in my teaching?

The following excerpt from the California English Language Arts/ English Development Instructional Framework illustrates how a group of teachers use interim assessment results to address some of the questions above:

> All incoming first graders in a school are assessed at the beginning of the school year on the foundational skills of the . . . ELA Standards, specifically, print concepts, phonological awareness, phonics and word recognition, and fluency. Results from their end-of-year kindergarten assessment are used to determine which sections of the assessment they receive. For example, if a student's results indicated a complete understanding of print concepts, that part of the assessment would be skipped, although close observations would be made during class to confirm last year's assessments. The teachers find the results from the beginning-of-the-year assessment to be a useful starting point for their instructional planning, particularly as students may have either lost or made up ground during the summer. In addition, the teachers assess, or obtain help to assess, the primary language foundational literacy skills of their ELs who are new to the school and use this information for instructional decision-making.
>
> The teachers continue to use the interim foundational skills assessments every six weeks as a gauge of progress. While the teachers are regularly using formative assessment practices during their instruction to gather evidence of students' skill development and to adjust instruction accordingly, they use the results of the interim assessments to monitor progress of individuals and the class as a whole, and to indicate to them where they need to make improvements in their teaching to ensure greater progress. The teachers also use the results as a means to evaluate and corroborate their own judgments about students' skill development in the period between the interim assessments' administration.[21]

With a clear understanding of the purposes of interim assessment, teachers and education leaders can use them to good effect. In the next section, we focus on the cautions educators need to pay attention to when using interim assessments specifically with ELLs.

PROCEEDING WITH CAUTION

ELL students will be measured on their academic content learning, reflected in the subject matter standards and aligned curricular learning goals, as well as on their English language use and development, reflected in ELP standards and aligned language-learning goals that correspond to subject matter practices. While this will likely occur using different assessments that target each set of learning goals, we know that an ELL's level of language proficiency will surely influence what she can demonstrate on the academic content assessment.

There needs to be appropriate correspondence across ELP and academic content standards as well as coherence in curricula and instructional practices designed to assist students to meet the standards. In other words, the ELP standards should describe the interpretive, productive, and collaborative uses of language needed to carry out disciplinary practices articulated in the academic content standards. If teachers appropriately target these uses of language—through carefully planning lessons and scaffolding generative, language-rich classroom practices—ELL students will develop in their language use over the course of the academic year.

As educators design or customize interim ELP assessments or interpret students' language use in content assessments, they need to identify the target language uses that correspond to the curricular goals and material students will be expected to engage with. Clarifying these disciplinary language uses helps to ensure that ELLs have multiple, scaffolded opportunities to employ these uses of language in their content learning.

Educators also need to consider what time frame is covered by academic interim assessments and how those assessment results may be used. Since ELLs' language competencies develop throughout the school year, they may have differential opportunities to learn and demonstrate subject-matter conceptual understandings and analytical practices within the school year. Such variations may lead to lower outcomes on interim assessments administered earlier in the school year. If interim assessment results are used for formative purposes—for example, to examine students' attainment of interim goals and inform curricular or instructional needs—teachers and school administrators can contextualize these results with evidence of students' developing English language proficiency using other classroom-based and ELP assessment results. However, if the interim assessment results have a high-stakes purpose—for example to summatively evaluate a student, program, teacher, or school—educators need to consider ELLs' developing English language proficiency. For instance, periodic "through-course" assessment results may be used to judge students' academic achievement after given periods, and these may be aggregated to form a final summative evaluation. Equally weighting these interim assessment results could easily misrepresent ELL students' learning, as doing so ignores how ELL students are differentially demonstrating their content learning across the school year as their use of English develops along with their conceptual understandings and analytical practices.[22]

The following vignette, focused on a middle-grades interim writing assessment (after six weeks of study) and associated rubric, illustrates how teachers make effective use of both ELP and content area evidence in order to reflect on intermediate goals, their planning and instructional efforts, and areas of strength and need in student learning.

———————— ◆ ————————

Examining Evidence of Informational Writing Skills from Interim Assessment

During the course of the fall quarter, students in Mr. Kim's class have been learning about informational writing. In addition to students who speak only English, his class includes a mixture of ELLs. Some students have very little English yet, others are at a more proficient level, and still others are well on their way to becoming very competent in English usage. The students have learned about the purpose and structure of the genre, and about how writers focus on a topic, group ideas together, use devices such as headings to distinguish subsections of information, provide examples to make a point, and include different kinds of information. In the context of learning about the structure and features of informational writing, students have also focused on the language of informational texts. This has included examining sentence and discourse structures to achieve clarity and cohesion. For example, students have studied how one piece of supporting information links to another through the use of transition words and phrases such as *another reason for, for example, in addition*, and *on the other hand*; they have also learned about expanding sentences to develop ideas and about the more formal register that informational writing requires to convey authority on the topic. Mr. Kim has used mentor texts from science and social studies sources throughout their study to exemplify the features of this genre and to stimulate analysis and discussion among his students of how authors achieve their informational writing goals. And of course, the students have had informational text writing assignments, progressively using the different structural and language features as they have been introduced. Because the students in his class exhibit a range of language proficiency, Mr. Kim has used the class discussions and student writing samples along the way to adjust his instruction and provide feedback so as to respond contingently to students' immediate needs. Students have also been involved in peer and self-assessment of their writing samples against the success criteria for each one, and have used their own feedback to improve their work.

After six weeks of study, all students at Mr. Kim's grade level are asked to write about a topic they have been studying in either social studies or science. They are provided with the scoring rubric developed by the teachers, which addresses all the purposes, structure, and language features they have been learning about, and makes explicit what they need to include in their written piece. Mr. Kim reviews the rubric with the students to ensure they understand the criteria.

Mr. Kim does not single out goals for his ELL students. They have been engaged with their English-proficient peers throughout this period of study and have learned about and worked with the same writing and understanding of the practices involved.

After the students have completed their writing, Mr. Kim uses the scoring rubric to evaluate his students' achievement. The grade-level teachers meet together to review the scores they have assigned and to examine several pieces of writing from across the grade level that have received the same score to ensure that they have been consistent in their application of the rubric.

Each teacher then presents an analysis of his or her class's strengths and needs. Among the strengths across the grade level are students' treatment of the topic and the use of linking phrases for the purpose of cohesion. An area that teachers would like to strengthen across the level is that of helping students more clearly understand that addition of extraneous information that the student might find interesting but that is irrelevant to the topic detracts from the writer's ability to maintain authority. In the case of ELLs specifically, a common need is for students to move from clause chaining with the use of conjunctions to producing sentences with relative clauses that use the pronouns *that* or *which*.

The teachers at Mr. Kim's grade level use this information to reflect on how they have taught informational writing and what changes they might make when they teach this form of writing again later in the year. They also consider the mentor texts they have used and the need to supplement these with texts that can address some of the areas of need they have identified. They also note that, going forward, they need to focus on embedding a focus on relative clauses in ELA content learning. As they recognize, even though this focus is intended to specifically address ELLs, it will benefit all students.

———————◆———————

Interim/benchmark assessments are used for summative purposes because, as their name suggests, they "sum up" a period of learning and are used to inform judgments about achievement at the end of that specific period. In the next section, we consider other summative assessments, particularly those that often claim most public attention because of the consequences for students associated with summative evaluative judgments.

SUMMATIVE ASSESSMENTS FOR HIGH-STAKES JUDGMENTS

There are two main kinds of assessments used for summative purposes that can have significant consequences for students: classroom-based summative assessments and large-scale assessments that are administered to all students, such as the end-of-year state tests. The latter can also have an impact on teachers, and indeed on schools, districts, or the state as a whole.

Classroom-based summative assessments can include graded end-of-lesson performances, midterm and final examinations, or culminating projects or portfolios used to inform period or course grades. Results from these kinds of assessments can lead to significant consequences, including a student's passing or failing a subject area course, being retained in grade, or having a sufficient grade point average (GPA) to qualify for college and career opportunities.

As their name suggests, large-scale assessments for summative purposes are administered to large cohorts of students, for example, all the students in a given grade, as in the case of state end-of-year assessments in ELA, math, and ELP. Such assessments are standardized because they are administered to all students, using the same procedures and in the same time frame. The following are among the questions to which teachers and administrators can find answers from these results:

- Who has met and who has not met the standards?
- What are the overall strengths and areas of need in students' learning?
- What are the strengths and areas of need in curricula, programs, and professional learning?
- Have the improvement strategies I/we put in place worked?

The answers to these questions can be a useful resource for improvement planning and resource allocation. Such large-scale assessment results can be aggregated so that state, district, and school leaders, as well as teachers, can look for patterns and trends in their students' performance that can shed light on needed improvements. The results can also be disaggregated to provide information on the relative performance of subgroups. This information can also provide guidance for improvement efforts.

However, as with some classroom-based assessments, the results from these assessments can also have far-reaching consequences for students, including determining whether a student receives a high school diploma and whether ELLs remain designated ELL or exit that status.

Because the stakes of a single assessment result can be very high, the technical quality of these assessments must also be very high. Technical quality refers to the *validity, reliability,* and *fairness* of the inferences drawn from the assessment results. *Validity* is the key issue in educational measurement and centers on whether an assessment is measuring what it is intended to measure and can serve well the intended purpose of the assessment. It is important to remember that validity always relates to a specific use of the assessment or the interpretation of evidence yielded by the assessment.

Reliability refers to how consistently an assessment measures what it is intended to measure. If a test is reliable, the results should be replicable. For instance, a change in the time of administration, day and time of scoring, who scores the assessment, and changes in the sample of assessment items should not create inconsistencies in results.

Fairness means that an assessment should permit students of both genders and diverse backgrounds to have an equal opportunity to demonstrate the skills and knowledge being assessed. With respect to ELLs, fairness also includes avoiding language that is unnecessarily complex in relation to the constructs the test is intended to measure.

All educators need to understand the specific inferences that any standardized large-scale test is intended to support. Those who develop tests are professionally obligated to clarify what inferences can and cannot be made from the results of their assessments. This kind of information should be available in the technical manual for the assessment and is often specified in score reports for students, parents, and teachers.

Educators must take special care in interpreting large-scale assessment results of ELL students. When educators examine ELLs' large-scale academic assessment outcomes, they also need to examine and interpret those results in light of ELL students' measured levels of English language proficiency.[23] When they do so, there is the potential to strengthen the signal from these results to more clearly understand student learning.

STRENGTHENING THE SIGNAL

Interpreting ELLs' performance on large-scale summative academic assessments administered in English presents a dilemma, traditionally framed as the following: If an ELL performs poorly on a content assessment, how can educators discern to what extent this is due to (1) insufficient English language proficiency to demonstrate content knowledge; (2) a lack of content knowledge or past opportunity to learn the content; (3) construct-irrelevant interference (e.g., unnecessarily complex language in the assessment); or (4) other sources of bias or error (e.g., cultural distance, rater misinterpretation)?[24] While these last two issues are largely the responsibility of test developers for demonstrating evidence of validity, reliability, and fairness, the first two issues rest more squarely within the domain of educators serving ELLs. In particular, as we have stressed throughout this chapter, knowing ELL students' levels of assessed English language proficiency can help to contextualize and interpret their academic assessment results. Equally important, since sophisticated language uses are inseparable from the opportunity to learn analytical practices and conceptual understandings described in the new standards, educators need to ensure that ELP and academic standards, learning opportunities, and assessments are rigorous, coherent, and aligned.

As we have noted throughout this book, the more explicit emphasis of college and career ready standards on the disciplinary uses of language needed to carry out subject matter practices, and the corresponding emphasis on such discourse-level practices in ELP standards, have led to ELP and content assessments that require students to demonstrate more sophisticated language use. This, in turn, increases the impact of language proficiency on academic performance. So, when educators examine ELLs' large-scale content assessment performance by their assessed levels of English language proficiency, they are more likely to identify system-level opportunities for change and improvement, such as priorities in adjusting curriculum design and teacher professional learning.

Equally important, because ELLs receiving quality instruction can develop conceptual understandings, analytical practices, and rigorous uses of language simultaneously, educators should define clear progress expectations for ELLs' English language proficiency development by time, and examine their academic progress and performance by ELP level and time in the system.[25] Such approaches to accountability, which local and state agencies are beginning to implement, send clearer signals to educators about the interrelationship of language and academic development, and can foster credibility and equity in accountability policies.[26] They also offer a more reasonable and useful evaluation of educational programs.

As new summative ELP and content assessments are implemented, educators can more effectively examine the relationships between these assessments and compare their findings with more frequent, classroom-based evidence gathered during the year to build a greater coherence in the assessment system for ELLs. This will help not only to more accurately measure ELL academic and linguistic progress and achievement, but also to use that information more effectively to evaluate and improve services and programs for ELLs.

In the next section, we continue the theme of strengthening the signal about ELLs' learning by highlighting some innovations in ELL assessment.

Innovations in Assessment for ELLs

Several innovations have been implemented to strengthen the signal we receive from ELLs' large-scale content assessments aligned to college and career ready standards. These include assessment development and review, assessment delivery, and assessment to determine ELL status. We discuss each of these innovations in turn.

TEST DEVELOPMENT AND REVIEW

Both the Partnership for the Assessment of Readiness for College and Careers (PARCC) consortium and Smarter Balanced Assessment Consortium (Smarter Balanced) have "tagged" their test items and tasks with a rating of language complexity, using a four-point rubric tool that describes levels of text density, language form and structure, and vocabulary.[27] This process has helped item/task developers and reviewers to better recognize the language demands required of students to respond to content assessment items. Also, field test responses from these assessments have been analyzed to understand how ELL students at different assessed ELP levels perform on items and tasks that target similar content area constructs using differing language complexity levels. This process has improved the initial development of items and tasks, and may eventually help test designers to more precisely measure ELLs' content domain knowledge with less construct-irrelevant language interference.[28] In particular, it can help ensure that computer-adaptive testing technologies do not underestimate ELLs' content knowledge through item assignment algorithms that confuse construct-irrelevant language complexity with content complexity.[29]

TEST DELIVERY

Smarter Balanced's usability, accessibility, and accommodations guidelines signaled a transformative advance in designated supports for ELLs in an online testing environment.[30] For example, teachers can authorize and designate for their ELL students supports such as online text-to-speech, translated test directions, glossary-like translations, or, for mathematics, full translations of test items into the student's home language. The latter may be particularly appropriate for students who enter the school system at the lowest levels of English language proficiency, have prior formal schooling in the home language or are being instructed bilingually, and may be able to demonstrate knowledge better using their home language. Also, the Smarter Balanced system embeds universal tools for all students, such as rest breaks and English dictionaries and glossaries that have previously been considered accommodations only for ELLs. They also offer embedded American Sign Language and Braille for students with disabilities that require these supports. Teachers and students are also provided practice test environments to better understand and gain facility with these tools before using them in live testing situations.

Traditionally, these kinds of tools have been unevenly available or inconsistently implemented within and across states. Now they are universally available and their use is standardized, with the result that they strengthen validity and reliability across testing environments.[31] Such tools help ELL students to demonstrate more fully and accurately what they know and can do. They also recognize students' primary languages as legitimate linguistic resources, foster educators' appreciation—and possibly more frequent use—of such learning supports, and reduce the misapplication and stigmatizing misperception of accommodations as unwarranted special treatment.

TEST USE IN DEFINING ELLS

As we noted earlier in the chapter, efforts have been made by a range of national, state, and local stakeholders to move toward a more common definition of ELL within and across states.[32] This effort has spawned a number of initiatives. For example, states and consortia have coordinated efforts to develop and implement enhanced home language surveys. Such surveys better gauge newly enrolling students' frequency of English and other language exposure and use across multiple environments in order to help educators more accurately identify potential ELLs.[33] States and consortia have also developed methods for comparing and validating initial ELP "screener" assessments (used to classify students as ELLs); procedures for making more consistent ELL classification decisions within and across states; and tools that "crosswalk" proficiency-level descriptors of different ELP standards. These tools help educators make reasonable comparisons of results across ELP assessments.[34]

With respect to determining the criteria that educators use to exit ELLs from the status, researchers have developed analytical tools to help determine an English-proficient performance standard on large-scale ELP assessments that take account of ELLs' academic content test performance, but that do not require a minimum level of academic test performance to be deemed English proficient.[35] Such methods are helping to identify a "sweet spot" range of assessed English language proficiency beyond which students perform no differently than comparable non-ELL students. This last innovation is particularly important, as many states continue to use performance criteria on academic content tests that native English-speaking students do not meet for reclassification decisions.[36]

Perhaps most important, groups of educators are developing and pilot-testing observational and evaluative protocols to assess the receptive and productive language uses ELLs need for successful engagement with grade-level content practices in the classroom, as well as for meeting social and occupational goals beyond school. These efforts may be aided by complementary work that is exploring learning progressions in academic disciplines (i.e, descriptions of how students gain increasing expertise within a discipline over time); disciplinary literacy; and dynamic language learning.[37] In addition, complex interpersonal communication, collaboration, and conflict resolution are among the many language-rich skills being explored as twenty-first-century competencies, and may be considered in locally developed performance assessments.[38] Over time, such tools may allow local educators within and across states to make more standardized and comparable judgments of ELLs' language proficiency. They may also replace nonstandardized and potentially construct-irrelevant criteria such as course grades. As educators develop, explore, and refine such tools, they also build their capacity to recognize and foster ELLs' disciplinary and social uses of language, and foster greater consistency and coherence in determining who is designated an ELL.

Clearly, strengthening assessment practices and tools and making more careful and appropriate use of assessment results are fundamental to improving teaching and learning for ELLs. As we have aimed to point out in this chapter, educators can take advantage of key leverage points, and carefully navigate key stress points, to foster a comprehensive and coherent assessment system for ELLs. Many innovations and developments are allowing teachers and students to use assessment *for* learning day by day, and to continually strengthen the signal from assessments *of* learning to better understand who ELLs are, how well they are progressing both linguistically and academically, and where improvements can be pursued. In the final chapter, we explore how policy can support (or discourage) strong pedagogy in language and content learning, formative assessment, and professional learning regarding ELLs, and we illustrate how teachers, educators, and policy makers can pursue and leverage policies to strengthen educator capacity to foster ELL students' success.

CHAPTER 6

◆

The Role of Policy

Fostering a Learning Culture for ELLs and Their Teachers

Throughout this book we have articulated a concrete vision of rigorous, contingent teaching and deep, transferable learning for students entering our schools as ELLs. In particular, we have illustrated how teachers can challenge and support students to develop simultaneously their conceptual understandings, analytical capacities, and disciplinary uses of language called for in more rigorous academic content and corresponding ELP standards. We have also enumerated several shifts in ELL pedagogy entailed by these standards and the learning sciences, and described how outdated or contradictory theoretical conceptions of second-language development often operate under the surface of teachers' current practices. We next have explained and illustrated how formative assessment, as assessment *for* learning, is a central pedagogical process that teachers and students use to obtain feedback and adjust ongoing teaching and learning. We have also described how assessment practices and outcomes define the ELL subgroup, the challenges associated with these practices and outcomes, and where they can and are being strengthened. Finally, we have defined and illustrated the appropriate uses of assessment *of* learning, which measures and evaluates a period of learning for formative or summative purposes.

In this final chapter we turn to policy implications of what we have laid out. Specifically, we will describe how policy plays a crucial role, intentionally or unintentionally, in supporting (or discouraging) the practices—pedagogical, collegial/collaborative, assessment, professional learning—that we have delineated to this point. Teachers, school and district administrators, and teacher educators cannot view themselves as passive recipients who are helpless in the face of policy. Rather, they are and should see themselves as key actors in developing, shaping, evaluating, improving, or replacing policies regarding education practices with ELLs that they enact daily in classrooms, schools, and districts.

How might policy support, and not undermine, the vision of teaching and learning we have described? What are some ways that educators can contribute productively and systematically to ensuring that local policies can support a culture of learning for ELLs as well as for school educators? What are the defining characteristics of a learning culture? First, a learning culture treats students and their teachers as lifelong learners, continuously growing through purposeful effort and supported by timely feedback. Second, it supports a collaborative learning environment, where teachers engage in dialogue and inquiry on problems of instructional practice. All educators participate, and supports are in place to ensure participation and risk taking. Third, it places the learner at the center: whether student or teacher, the learner is actively engaged in making meaning, receiving feedback, reflecting on his or her practice, and being supported to take charge of his or her own learning.[1]

First let us consider what most educators associate with the word *policy*. Very likely it is large external mandates from a level of government that is far removed from their daily practice. For example, the No Child Left Behind (NCLB) Act's Title I Adequate Yearly Progress accountability provisions, defined in law in 2002, set the expectation that 100 percent of the millions of educationally disadvantaged students served under Title I would be proficient in English language arts and mathematics by 2014, regardless of their starting point or amount of time in the system![2] Or perhaps it is state-level high school graduation requirements, which use high-stakes high school graduation or end-of-course tests or grade point averages to determine which students will receive diplomas and which will not. With respect to ELLs, it could be NCLB Title III, which requires increasing percentages of ELLs who are provided services with Title III funds to regularly progress in their English development and to attain at some point (defined by time in the program, but not by initial language proficiency or grade level) "English proficient" on an ELP test.[3] It could also be instructional program mandates such as those enacted under California's Proposition 227, or similar laws passed by voters in Arizona and Massachusetts, which severely restrict the classroom teacher's use of bilingual instructional methods. What is clear in these examples of policy is that educators have not been involved in their development; these policies have been generated outside of the education profession and imposed from the outside in. Yet they largely define how educational effectiveness is to be measured, and virtually always specify sanctions for noncompliance and missing the performance target, and occasionally, rewards for meeting the target.

Closer to home, educators may also consider local policies enacted by their school boards and district leadership. These often address implementation of state and federal policies, but they can also set very consequential courses of action for how curriculum will be developed, how teaching and learning will be carried out in schools, how professional learning will be organized and supported, and how teacher and school administrator performance standards will be defined and evaluated. While school-based educators may have more of a say in local policy development, many still find that policies are developed and enacted based on personal theories and outdated notions that have little connection to their day-to-day problems of practice and professional lives.

Policy as a Course of Action Encoding Values

A less obvious but crucial way to view policy is as a prescribed course of action that encodes key values of those that make and enact policy prescriptions. Importantly, most policies are formed and operate under a theory of action that reflects a particular view of what the problem is, and how a policy will address the problem through some causal chain that is itself informed by theories—for example, of how students learn language. As we saw in chapter 3, for example, there are many outdated theories of second-language development under which teachers still operate, and such theories are often reflected in and reinforced by existing policies. Also, as we saw in chapter 5, statutes and case law designed to protect the civil rights of national origin and linguistic minority students can unintentionally reflect a deficit orientation toward such students that communicates itself through corresponding policy. The very notion of "sheltered" content instruction described in chapter 3, for example, suggests a protective purpose—sheltering students from what?—and contributes to a focus on what students don't have and cannot do, as opposed to what linguistic, cultural, and cognitive capacities and funds of knowledge they bring to, and can utilize in, the process of learning.

At the other extreme, some policies may be based on no research evidence, but instead appeal to commonsense notions that are overly simplistic and contradicted by evidence. California's Proposition 227, approved by voters in 1998, and Arizona's Proposition 203, approved by voters in 2000, for example, made blanket claims that ELL students should learn English "in a period not normally expected to exceed one year," and mandated classroom instructional methodologies via the ballot box. In particular, Arizona's 2006 revised statute requires Arizona educators to implement a four-hour block of English language development in which ELLs receive explicit discrete-language-skills instruction (with time allotments for each skill), and thereby narrows the curriculum and instruction into a de facto sequence of language first, content later.[4]

Policy also channels financial and human resources in particular directions, and the incentive system set up largely influences how adults behave in the system, and by extension, what experiences students can expect to have as a result. While policies may in principle be based on some form of research evidence, they seldom consider the context of existing strengths and assets, other practices and policies, the capacity of adults in the system to carry out the prescribed actions, or what supports will be required. As Richard Elmore has long noted, one cannot expect improved performance in public education without strengthening the capacity of those who are closest to students' daily learning. And strengthening this capacity to support students' learning requires not just behavioral incentives, but focused and sustained supports to improve the pedagogical practices of teachers and the learning tactics of students in the classroom, and larger systems of support for building professional culture.[5] There is consensus that the professional culture of schools is generally (and ironically) not one that supports adult professional learning and growth. Why has this been so, and what role has policy contributed to this? We explore this next.

"Policy is the Problem"—The Underlying Dynamic of K–12 School Reform Policy

After forty years of involvement in education policy for school reform, Richard Elmore recently reflected that he used to think policy was the solution, but now he thinks policy is the problem.[6] This startling observation provokes us to think about why policy makers so strongly dictate the practices of educators, more so than for any other professional group. The underlying problems of K–12 public education policy have historical roots that have been explored by scholars and journalists. Jal Mehta observes that teaching was institutionalized as a semiprofession in the early twentieth century and was situated within a hierarchically administered bureaucracy, one that leaves teachers and schools at the bottom of an increasingly long chain of implementation of the ideas of politicians, external reformers, and central office managers disconnected from the reality of daily pedagogical practice.[7] Given a very weak professional culture, teachers are often placed in the position of factory workers, subject to external controls and external accountability. The efforts of school reformers, whether operating from a civil rights perspective or from a market competition orientation, have been largely focused on controlling teacher behavior from outside through policies and regulations, with little appreciation of the need to develop a professional culture centered on problems of instructional practice.[8]

This dynamic has led over time to a downward cycle of deprofessionalization: high external control and external accountability on narrow indicators and compliance; low autonomy, low prestige, little support, low pay, and difficult working conditions. In particular, for the last twelve years under NCLB, teachers have experienced further diminished autonomy, and have had to implement increasingly narrow, scripted curricula and pacing guides. They have been required to rely largely on standardized annual tests emphasizing factual recall over critical thinking and literacy that are of little pedagogical use and have served to distort the goals of teaching and to largely trivialize learning. While test-based accountability has shined a spotlight on disaggregated group performance, including that of ELLs, it has also narrowed the view of what is educationally meaningful to that which can be easily measured. And as noted in the last chapter, even subgroup performance reporting for ELLs ignores the revolving door phenomenon generated by current definitional policies, and grossly underreports these students' actual progress and attainment.

At the same time, we are currently in an era of great transformation and potential promise for strengthening instructional capacity and learning opportunities. The new standards in English language arts, math, and science, along with corresponding ELP standards, represent a significant improvement over past standards in terms of their coherence across grade levels and their clearer articulation of conceptual understandings, disciplinary analytical practices, and language uses. These standards are the current instantiation of what should be applied and continuously improved on in rigor, precision, and meaningful use. We are also gaining a greater understanding of how people learn, and these advances in learning sciences have expanded our ability to recognize and foster deep learning that can be adapted and transferred to novel situations.[9] Yet, while we have developed a greater understanding of knowing what students know, we still have mostly rhetorical support for more comprehensive and coherent assessment systems. In light of the demands of the new standards, and the profound inadequacy of NCLB-era large-scale assessments of learning, there is a growing sense of the need to equally value assessment *for* learning in addition to improving assessment *of* learning. How can policy be used to leverage these intellectual insights, pedagogical resources, and potential openings to foster a learning culture in schools?

There is a growing awareness that in order to strengthen a learning culture for all students, especially ELL students and their teachers, we need to flip the prevailing paradigm of school improvement.[10] That is, instead of attempting to improve instructional practice from the outside in with external mandates and controls, we need to create knowledge and cultivate expert practice from within local settings. To the extent that knowledge is created by and in collaboration with teachers and school leaders focused on key problems of practice, teachers are not passive agents implementing the ideas of others, but rather are practicing professionals who create and develop the complex knowledge and practices of their field.[11]

Doing so will clearly involve developing what Hargreaves and Fullan call professional capital.[12] What does this mean for teachers? Professional capital comes as a result of cultivating human, social, and decisional capital. Human capital means teachers have and continually develop a deep knowledge of their subject matter, know how their students learn and build on their assets and strengths, cultivate pedagogical expertise, have empathy for students, families, and colleagues, and demonstrate commitment to continually improving practice. Cultivating human capital implies strengthening teacher preservice preparation and in-service professional learning.

Social capital means teachers do not work in isolation on these dimensions, but open up their practice and collaborate with colleagues within and across schools to support each other's learning over long periods of time. Cultivating social capital is critical for sustaining professional development and learning, and in fact requires that adults use sociocultural approaches to learning, described in chapter 3 and stressed throughout this book.

Decisional capital means teachers make informed pedagogical judgments based on accumulated experience, sustained expert practice, and reflection. Cultivating decisional capital is effectively accomplished through the practices of formative assessment as we have described them, because these practices strengthen teachers' expert judgment of where students are in their learning and how they can be helped to move forward. Decisional capital is also enhanced through interaction with committed colleagues, the social and human capital referenced above.

School districts that value and cultivate professional capital (such as the one Ms. Cardenas, from chapter 1, works in) are better able to develop what Mehta envisions as communities of talented, committed, and growing practitioners functioning in schools that are centers of inquiry. Educators in these schools work as a community of practice, supporting and holding each other accountable for continually improving that practice in ways that are responsive to the strengths and needs of their students. This practice of internal accountability—opening up practice to observation and respectful, formative critique; pushing one another forward and holding each other accountable to develop practices that demonstrably advance student learning—is a widely recognized characteristic of successful schools and districts.[13] And as teachers and administrators develop internal accountability, they are more strongly positioned to call for reciprocal accountability from local policy makers; that is, to demand the resources, supports, and discretional decision making needed to build further the capacity that improves practice.

This infrastructure to support continual improvement in schools extends outward to administrators, who also need practice at becoming change managers who help teachers clarify and design changes in curriculum and pedagogy, and who set the pace of implementation.[14] As one master teacher has observed, "The principal's class is her teachers."[15] For site administrators to help their teachers develop, they, too, will require professional development. Hence there is a concurrent need for coherence among professional learning standards for teachers and administrators.

Policies That Promote a Culture of Learning for Implementing College and Career Ready Standards

The new college and career ready standards have triggered a profound, cascading, and systemic change that requires new curriculum frameworks and instructional materials; teacher and administrator preparation, professional learning practices, and evaluation; and assessment and accountability systems. As one California education policy maker summed up the effect of implementing the new standards on state policy making, "This changes almost everything."[16] Even in states with little or no political controversy surrounding the new standards, local educators are being significantly challenged in their capacity to implement curriculum, instruction, and assessment that fosters the deep learning called for by the new standards.[17] This challenge has also revealed the fundamental weaknesses of the NCLB-based system that has been in place for the last dozen years: narrow, scripted curricula, "teacher-proof" materials, pacing guides, standardized large-scale tests of factual recall, and high-stakes test-based accountability that incentivizes test preparation and gaming. Most of these features of the education system are incompatible with what the new standards—and indeed life and work in the twenty-first century—require of educators and students. As a result, education leaders are rediscovering that pedagogy and learning are the heart of the educational matter. Teachers are being newly recognized as instructional decision makers, and local administrators are being expected to lead enormous efforts to create support and engagement structures appropriate to the new standards' more ambitious teaching and learning goals.[18]

Teachers need to play an active and central role in strengthening their profession to realize the potential of all students, and particularly ELLs. In what ways can they realistically participate in establishing and strengthening policies, systems, and practices that build the teaching profession, improve conditions for adult apprenticeship and learning, and cultivate the learning culture ELL students need and deserve? How can school and district administrators create the right conditions and supports for strengthening instructional leadership? We next explore four key strands of policy where teachers and school administrators can actively work to strengthen pedagogy and assessment through enacting policy and practices: (1) professional learning; (2) teacher preparation; (3) assessment literacy; and (4) teacher evaluation.[19]

PROFESSIONAL LEARNING

Clearly, teachers must advocate for and commit to enacting new modes of in-service professional learning that are focused on authentic problems of practice and that help to build a professional learning culture. Such professional learning supports teachers to identify priorities and pathways for their own pedagogical development. It uses coaching and facilitated discussions to help teachers set learning goals, plan, and elicit and use evidence of learning during teaching and learning, and it encourages teachers to reflect on their practice and develop ways of engaging students in deeper inquiry and metacognition. In fact, professional learning of this kind mirrors the very practices teachers need to employ with their students to empower them as learners. Such practices take time and effort to enact, as they challenge the "sit-and-get" transmission models of professional development that many teachers often experience.[20]

This more rigorous professional learning depends in large part on teachers' engaging in deep collegial dialogue, using collaborative norms that reflect an inquiry stance and a growth mindset. As Nelson and her colleagues note, rather than engaging in superficially congenial conversations that stay on the surface of instructional practice and seek to avoid affective conflict, collegial dialogues use a cycle of questioning, gathering of and reflecting on evidence, and cognitive conflict to negotiate meaning, make informed decisions, and take action.[21] Whether designing a lesson or assessment together, collaboratively analyzing student work, or clarifying the meaning of learning goals or standards, teachers need practice and support to employ collegial dialogues grounded in substantive questions to drive deeper conversations in teacher inquiry groups. For example, in examining instructional practices, they may ask each other:

- Why are these meaningful learning goals? What will students say, do, make, or write as a result?
- How might engagement participation structures be adjusted to promote more focused dialogue?
- If we teach this concept differently, what implications are there for students' understanding? What scaffolds should be used to support students' analytical practices and language uses?

Regarding learning expectations represented in student work, they may ask each other:

- When students understand this concept or analytical practice, what will it sound or look like? What language will students use to carry out the practices or demonstrate understanding of key concepts? How can we best support this language use?
- What misconceptions might we expect to see in student work? How might these be manifested in students' explanations, reasoning, and selection of evidence?

In identifying patterns in student work, teachers might ask:

- What do we see or hear that suggests students understand/almost understand/do not understand? Which students are these, and what does that tell us?
- How are students manifesting their understandings in speech or writing? How does their language use evolve with their conceptual understandings and analytical practices?

In connecting student work to practice, teachers may ask:

- Do students' responses show that students' communicative abilities are developing?
- Why did I/we teach it this way? Are there other options? Should I/ we continue, make some modifications, or try a different approach?[22]

Of course, site administrators will also need to shift their practice to become facilitative leaders of strengthening teaching and learning. Teachers and school administrators can work with local education leaders to design and put into place support and engagement structures that help apprentice teachers and facilitate learning communities to support cross-role and job-alike school teams collaborating on problems of pedagogical practice.

TEACHER PREPARATION

In order to build instructional capacity in schools for enacting the kinds of practices we have described in prior chapters, educators also need to contribute to strengthening teacher preparation and induction. Preservice teachers need foundational understandings and guided experiences employing powerful pedagogical and formative assessment practices.[23] This includes developing content pedagogy that incorporates an understanding of the key concepts, analytical practices, and language uses of the disciplines. It also includes pedagogical language knowledge focusing on discipline-specific language uses within content area practices, and language development strategies for teaching ELLs with applications within the disciplines being taught.[24] In fact, this is where outdated conceptions of second-language development, as described in chapter 3, can be examined and new conceptions that are more consonant with deep learning of conceptual understandings, analytical practices, and language uses reflected in the new standards can be explored.

But preservice teachers also benefit from a "clinical curriculum" that directly ties coursework to fieldwork. Such teacher education classes "engage novices in assessing students, designing lessons, trying out strategies, evaluating outcomes, and continuously reflecting with expert guidance on what they are learning" with cooperating teachers and supervisors chosen for their pedagogical and formative assessment expertise.[25]

What role might local teacher leaders, teacher educators, and school leaders play in supporting this shift in teacher preparation and induction policies to enable these practices? First, local policy makers and education leaders can signal they value teachers committed to engaging in these deeper pedagogical practices by recruiting from teacher preparation programs that develop teachers' capacity to engage in them. Second, teacher leaders, instructional coaches, and master teachers can also partner locally with such programs to support clinical experiences and mentorship for preservice teachers.

Of course, teacher preparation and induction is also a state-level policy issue (as state requirements should address these needed competencies in teacher preparation, credentialing, induction, and support), as are administrator credentialing requirements. Teacher preparation and credentialing systems can incorporate stronger pedagogical and formative assessment practices into the learning objectives of all preservice and induction-level teachers, and foster support, feedback, and cultivation of these practices via clinical teaching and mentorship. Administrator credentialing programs can incorporate training to develop understanding and practice in skillful feedback and mentoring of teachers' pedagogical and formative assessment practices.

ASSESSMENT LITERACY

As we have emphasized throughout the book, particularly in chapters 4 and 5, strengthening pedagogical practices for ELLs requires that everyone—teachers, school and district administrators, parents, policy makers, and other stakeholders—better understand the varying purposes and appropriate (and inappropriate) uses of different forms of assessment evidence. Developing assessment literacy is nowhere more important than with respect to formative assessment, or assessment *for* learning. In the United States, educators and the public strongly associate assessment with testing. Because of this, formative assessment as a pedagogical process composed of practices that teachers and students engage in during teaching and learning has generally been underrecognized and underutilized.

As teaching and learning become the central focus of implementing the new standards, formative assessment needs to be a privileged and prioritized part of any comprehensive assessment system. As we have also seen, formative assessment is essential in teaching ELLs, because it requires teachers and students to engage in purposeful interaction to make meaning. It also strengthens reflection and feedback for students and teachers, scaffolds learner autonomy, and develops students' academic uses of language while they engage in conceptual and analytical work.

How can local educators help to ensure that formative assessment is properly understood and recognized as essential to teachers' pedagogical practice? First, and perhaps most difficult, they must ensure that the formative assessment is not mischaracterized as a test or event or bank of test items. (One clear indicator of its not being seen as a coherent set of pedagogical practices is the use of the plural, as in "formative assessments.") School and district leaders must be clear about what formative assessment means and provide sustained support to foster it.[26]

There are encouraging signs that formative assessment can be properly incorporated into efforts to implement larger state standards. For example, California's recent English language arts/English language development (ELA/ELD) curriculum and instruction framework prominently features short-cycle formative assessment as a central teacher practice within its comprehensive assessment system, with clearly articulated and appropriate uses for this and for intermediate interim/benchmark assessment and summative classroom and large-scale assessment. This coherence is the result of an inclusive, transparent public process that California education policy makers engaged in, with strong representation from teachers, teacher leaders, local and state administrators and policy makers, professional development providers, and researchers. A large multitiered statewide system of professional learning support has been helping regional and local educators to understand and begin implementing these practices.

As local educators design and implement professional development plans, they need to explicitly define their conceptions of student engagement, motivation, and learning, and critically examine proposed assessment practices and uses against these conceptions. Teachers and local education leaders must also critically examine any formative assessment "tools" and professional development resources for formative assessment. What are the conceptions of learning underlying these resources, and how well do these resources align with and support local curricular/learning goals as well as key practices of the formative assessment process?

Finally, developing assessment literacy requires educators to ensure that professional development and explanatory materials and reports created for key audiences (teachers, board members, parents, students) clearly describe appropriate and inappropriate uses of each assessment component in their systems. In particular, as explained in chapter 5, summative assessment results designed for system-level evaluation purposes should not be used for instructional decisions regarding individual students, as these assessments are not sensitive or fine grained enough for that purpose. Also, interim/benchmark assessments that purport to evaluate learning after a period of time should accurately target the objectives taught in the preceding time period. And contextualizing outcomes of ELLs using their assessed levels of English language proficiency, as illustrated earlier, is particularly critical. Appropriate use of multiple forms of assessment evidence is essential to developing more nuanced and responsive accountability systems for ELL students and their educators. There is no shortage of thoughtful guidance on this, and there is some evidence that states are refining their accountability systems to be more responsive and meaningful for educators and the public.[27]

TEACHER EVALUATION

Perhaps no other area of policy can support or undermine effective pedagogical practices and formative assessment more than that of teacher evaluation. In fact, teacher evaluation has become a controversial public policy issue, as many policy makers and education reformers have proposed using annual test scores as the metric by which teacher effectiveness is judged.[28] Yet, if approached from a different perspective, the entire teacher evaluation process can become powerfully supportive of the pedagogical practices and the formative assessment process teachers need to develop. So how can teachers and local administrators work toward enacting teacher evaluation policy that supports strong pedagogical practice, particularly formative assessment, and that contributes to a learning culture?

First, they need to work together with local policy makers to incorporate into teacher evaluation systems teacher observation protocols and student survey instruments that value and capture formative assessment practices, and help teachers and students improve in enacting them. As a result of rigorous empirical-research evidence, teacher evaluation policy is expanding its initial focus on student test scores to include a broader set of measures in order to strengthen reliability, validity, and relevance of teacher evaluation systems.[29]

Strong evidence supports including multiple observations of teacher practice over time by trained peers with opportunities for actionable formative feedback and self-reflection—both of which mirror the formative assessment process.[30] Evidence also supports including student perception surveys that reflect the theory of instruction defining expectations for teachers in the system, and that elicit student experiences of their teachers' expectations, support, and feedback.[31]

Carefully incorporating student feedback on these dimensions into teacher evaluation is a powerful way to support student-centered formative assessment practices. It also strengthens reciprocal accountability between education policy makers and teachers for instructional capacity building and expected performance.[32] This is the case because student surveys help to evaluate support systems for teachers as much as they diagnose pedagogical needs.[33]

Educators must also ensure that implementing and evaluating formative assessment entails more than a simple walk-through checklist of evidence-based practices. In fact, a checklist approach can unintentionally undermine authentic formative assessment by emphasizing superficial implementation over a deeper observational approach with feedback that can promote a more responsive adaptation of formative assessment practices to local needs and contexts.[34] To do this, local educators can look to strong examples from states that have convened educators, community stakeholders, and researchers to develop teacher and administrator performance standards and indicators that value and coherently incorporate formative assessment and other key pedagogical practices.

In Nevada, for example, teacher high-leverage instructional standards specify that students engage in meaning making through discourse, and have indicators that focus on teachers structuring classroom environments to enable collaboration and provide opportunities for extended productive discourse between teacher and student and among students. Another standard explicitly calls for assessment to be integrated into instruction, and its indicators examine key characteristics of formative assessment practice. Also, teacher professional responsibilities standards include probing student perceptions as well as reflecting on professional growth and practice.

Interestingly, Nevada has a set of parallel administrator high-leverage instructional leadership standards that include creating and sustaining a focus on learning, continuous improvement, and productive relationships.[35] Such frameworks bring greater coherence to teacher and administrator collaboration, and support mutually strengthened practices and greater effectiveness and improvement. Teachers and local administrators can examine and adapt such exemplary models as they develop or refine local standards and indicators.

In the end, as teachers and school administrators engage actively in the reformulation of pedagogical, curricular, and assessment practices as we have discussed throughout this book, they will also necessarily engage in reviewing, critiquing, responding to, and transforming local and possibly state policies. This is not "becoming political" or "playing politics." Rather, it is insisting on and demonstrating a responsible and responsive professionalism, and taking greater ownership for improving teaching and learning.

If teachers, teacher leaders, local administrators, and teacher educators do not clarify what it is they need to improve, someone largely removed from the day-to-day reality of schools will likely do so. Given the sophisticated language demands inherent in the new content standards, all students need rich learning environments that provide them with high challenge and high support to grapple with concepts and analytical practices as they are developing language. Our laws, policies, and civil-rights-protected class provisions drive us to dichotomous categories, but the teaching and assessment practices and learning opportunities we provide students (whether ELL, former ELL, emergent bilingual, multilingual, monolingual, or Standard English Learner) should be potent, coherent, and continuously growing.

Notes

Chapter 1

1. Grace Kena et al., *The Condition of Education 2014* (NCES 2014-083) U.S. Department of Education, National Center for Education Statistics (Washington, DC, 2014), http://nces.ed.gov/pubs2014/2014083.pdf; Stella M. Flores, Jeanne Batalova, and Michael Fix, *The Educational Trajectories of English Language Learners in Texas* (Washington, DC: Migration Policy Institute, 2012).
2. Claude Goldenberg, "Teaching English Language Learners: What the Research Does—and Does Not—Say," *American Educator* 32, no. 2 (2008): 8–23, 42–44.
3. Kena et al., *The Condition of Education.*
4. Note also that the very measurement of achievement gaps between ELL and non-ELL students is problematic, given the instability of the ELL cohort as typically defined. This issue is explored in chapter 5.
5. Kena et al., *The Condition of Education.*
6. See James W. Pellegrino and Margaret L. Hilton, eds., *Education for Life and Work: Developing Transferable Knowledge and Skills in the 21st Century* (Washington, DC: The National Academies Press, 2012).
7. National Governors Association Center for Best Practices and Council of Chief State School Officers, *Common Core State Standards for English Language Arts and Literacy in History/Social Studies, Science, and Technical Subjects* (Washington, DC: Authors, 2010); National Governors Association Center for Best Practices and Council of Chief State School Officers, *Common Core State Standards for Mathematics* (Washington, DC: Authors, 2010); NGSS Lead States, *Next Generation Science Standards: For States, By States* (Washington, DC: The National Academies Press, 2013); Council of Chief State School Officers, *Framework for English Language Proficiency*

Development Standards Corresponding to the Common Core State Standards and the Next Generation Science Standards (Washington, DC: CCSSO, 2012); California Department of Education, "English Language Development Standards," http://www.cde.ca.gov/sp/el/er/eldstandards.asp; California Department of Education, "English-Language Arts/English Language Development Curriculum and Instruction Framework," http://www.cde.ca.gov/ci/rl/cf/elaeldfrmwrksbeadopted.asp.

8. Helen Quinn, Okhee Lee, and Guadalupe Valdés, "Language Demands and Opportunities in Relation to Next Generation Science Standards for English Language Learners: What Teachers Need to Know," in *Understanding Language: Commissioned Papers on Language and Literacy Issues in the Common Core State Standards and Next Generation Science Standards*, ed. Kenji Hakuta and María Santos (Palo Alto, CA: Stanford University, 2012), 32–43.

9. Judit Moschkovich, "Mathematics, the Common Core, and Language: Recommendations for Mathematics Instruction for ELs Aligned with the Common Core," in *Understanding Language* (see note 8), 17–31.

10. George C. Bunch, Amanda Kibler, and Susan Pimentel, "Realizing Opportunities for English Learners in the Common Core English Language Arts and Disciplinary Literacy Standards," in *Understanding Language* (see note 8), 1–16.

11. Deborah J. Short and Shannon Fitzsimmons, *Double the Work: Challenges and Solutions to Acquiring Language and Academic Literacy for Adolescent English Language Learners—A Report to Carnegie Corporation of New York* (Washington, DC: Alliance for Excellent Education, 2007).

12. Margaret Heritage, Aída Walqui, and Robert Linquanti, "Formative Assessment as Contingent Teaching and Learning: Perspectives on Assessment *As* and *For* Language Learning in the Content Areas" (paper prepared for the Understanding Language Initiative, Stanford University, May 2013, ell.Stanford.edu/policy).

13. Bunch et al., "Realizing Opportunities for English Learners"; Moschkovich, "Mathematics, the Common Core, and Language"; Quinn et al., "Language Demands and Opportunities"; Leo van Lier and Aída Walqui, "Language and the Common Core State Standards," in *Understanding Language* (see note 8), 44–51.

14. "Intermediate" is a descriptor applied to students' performance level on English language development (ELD) assessments. For example, according to one ELD assessment, intermediate students can understand some complex vocabulary and syntax, with occasional gaps in comprehension. They can follow some complex, multistep oral directions, and use a range of vocabulary and syntax appropriate to setting and purpose, with gaps in communication. They can tell a coherent story using phrases and incomplete

sentences. They can use their knowledge of grammar and mechanics to identify appropriate words or phrases to complete a sentence. Their writing may contain errors in grammar, vocabulary, and/or syntax, while their compositions have a disorganized sequence of events, containing some details and repetitive transitional words; George C. Bunch, "Pedagogical Language Knowledge: Preparing Mainstream Teachers for English Learners in the New Standards Era," *Review of Research in Education* 37, no. 1 (2013): 298–341.

15. We note grade 6–12 literacy standards for history/social studies are specified under the Common Core State Standards in English Language Arts.

16. Lev S. Vygotsky, *Mind and Society: The Development of Higher Mental Processes* (Cambridge, MA: Harvard University Press, 1978).

17. Alison L. Bailey, Margaret Heritage, and Frances A. Butler, "Developmental Considerations and Curricular Contexts in the Assessment of Young Language Learners," in *The Companion to Language Assessment*, ed. Antony John Kunnan (New York: Wiley-Blackwell Press, 2014), 421–439.

18. The story and the language samples are taken from an actual third-grade classroom in Los Angeles.

19. Allan Collins, John S. Brown, and Ann Holum, "Cognitive Apprenticeship: Making Thinking Visible," *American Educator* 15, no. 3 (1991): 1–18.

20. Margaret Heritage, *Formative Assessment in Practice* (Cambridge, MA: Harvard University Press, 2013).

21. Leo van Lier, *The Ecology and Semiotics of Language Learning: A Sociocultural Perspective* (Dordrecht, NL: Kluwer Academic Press, 2004).

22. John Lyons, *Introduction to Theoretical Linguistics* (Cambridge: Cambridge University Press, 1968).

23. Next Generation Science Standards, ehttp://www.nextgenscience.org/search-performance-expectations?tid_2%5B%5D=13.

24. Unless otherwise noted, teachers' real names are used in the vignettes and pseudonyms are used for the children.

25. In this book we conceive of scaffolding not merely as "help" provided to students to assist them in completing a momentary task or to preteach the content of a text, but rather as supports specifically designed to induce students' development and increase their autonomy. Scaffolding is discussed more fully in chapter 2.

26. Jean Lave, *Cognition in Practice: Mind, Mathematics and Culture in Everyday Life* (New York: Cambridge University Press, 1988).

27. Heritage, *Formative Assessment in Practice*.

28. Ibid.

29. Alexei Leontiev, quoted in Urie Bronfenbrenner, *The Ecology of Human Development* (Cambridge, MA: Harvard University Press, 1979), 40.

Chapter 2

1. These suggestions draw on work by Aída Walqui and her colleagues at the Understanding Language initiative at Stanford University, a group of educators formed in 2012 to inform educators nationwide on the implementation of college and career ready standards with ELLs.

2. Aída Walqui, Nanette Koelsch, and Mary Schmida, "Persuasion Across Time and Space: Analyzing and Producing Complex Texts." ell.Stanford.edu

3. James G. Greeno, Allan M. Collins, and Lauren B. Resnick, "Cognition and Learning," in *Handbook of Educational Psychology*, ed. David C. Berliner and Robert C. Calfee (New York: Macmillan, 1996), 15–46; John Seely Brown, Allan M. Collins, and Paul Duguid, "Situated Cognition and the Culture of Learning," *Educational Researcher* 18, no. 1 (1989): 32–42.

4. James P. Lantolf and Steven L. Thorne, *Sociocultural Theory and the Genesis of Second Language Development* (Oxford, UK: Oxford University Press, 2006); Jean Lave and Etienne Wenger, *Situated Learning: Legitimate Peripheral Participation* (Cambridge: Cambridge University Press, 1991); Leo van Lier, *The Ecology and Semiotics of Language Learning: A Sociocultural Perspective* (Dordrecht, NL: Kluwer Academic Press, 2004).

5. NGSS Lead States, *Next Generation Science Standards: For States, By States* (Washington, DC: The National Academies Press, 2013).

6. Urie Bronfenbrenner and Stephen J. Ceci, "Nature-Nurture Reconceptualized in Developmental Perspective: A Bioecological Model," *Psychological Review* 101, no. 4 (1994): 568–586; Edward L. Deci and Richard Flaste, *Why We Do What We Do: The Dynamics of Personal Autonomy* (New York: Putnam's Sons, 1995).

7. See, for example, Gladys Jean and Daphnée Simard, "Grammar Teaching and Learning in L2: Necessary, but Boring?" *Foreign Language Annals* 44, no. 3 (2011): 467–494; Diane Larsen-Freeman, "Research into Practice: Grammar Learning and Teaching," *Language Teaching* (in preparation); Henry G. Widdowson, *Learning Purpose and Language Use* (Oxford, UK: Oxford University Press, 1983).

8. In the introduction to beginning ESL materials developed for the New York City Department of Education, Guadalupe Valdés, Amanda Kibler, and Maneka Brooks, as part of their theory of action, state that "Students' primary language has a strong role in educating students and can be used effectively to supplement development in listening, speaking, reading and writing." Later on, they say that students' first language is to be used as "just in time aid" in the learning of English, a suggestion followed by Ms. Warren. *Unit 1 of Beginning ESL Units for Middle and High School: Theoretical and Pedagogical Foundations* (New York: New York City Department of Education, 2014), 2.

9. See, for example, the discussion of the concept in Gordon Wells, *Dialogic Inquiry: Towards a Socio-cultural Practice and Theory of Education* (Cambridge: Cambridge University Press, 1999).

10. Leo van Lier, "From Input to Affordance: Social-interaction Learning from an Ecological Perspective," in *Sociocultural Theory and Second Language Learning*, ed. James Lantolf (Oxford, UK: Oxford University Press, 2000), 246.

11. Ibid.

12. In a study of why the teaching of grammar in isolation is neither useful—although perceived as necessary—nor interesting, Gladys Jean and Daphnée Simard write: "Grammar instruction is perceived by both students and teachers as necessary and effective, but not as something they enjoy doing" ("Grammar Teaching and Learning in L2," 467).

13. In his influential book, *Schoolteacher: A Sociological Study*, Dan Lortie suggested the term "apprenticeship of observation" as the perseverance of teaching practices informed by their own learning experiences (Chicago: University of Chicago Press, 1975).

14. Ann Fadiman, *The Spirit Catches You and You Fall Down* (New York: Farrar Straus and Giroux, 1997), 154–155.

15. Ann Fadiman, *The Spirit Catches You and You Fall Down*, 155.

16. Aída Walqui, "Persuasion Across Time and Space: Analyzing and Producing Complex Texts," Stanford University Graduate School of Education, http://ell.stanford.edu/teaching_resources/ela.

17. For a good description of school genres and their components, see Beverly M. Derewianka and Pauline T. Jones, *Teaching Language in Context* (Melbourne, AU: Oxford University Press, 2012).

18. "Look, kids, there are words which in English are called cognates. These words look very similar in English and other languages derived from Greek or Latin, and they tend to be important words in the development of disciplinary practices. When you read a text, review it to see if you detect any cognates, because they can be very useful. For example, *composition* and *composición*, *relevance* and *relevancia*, and *structure* and *estructura* are cognates in English and Spanish."

19. See, for example, James W. Pellegrino and Margaret L. Hilton, eds., *Education for Life and Work: Developing Transferable Knowledge and Skills in the 21st Century* (Washington, DC: The National Academies Press, 2012).

20. This group currently constitutes the largest segment of the population of ELLs, and it is also the fastest-growing group.

21. This case is based on one of the protagonists of Michael Paul Mason's *Head Cases: Stories of Brain Injury and Its Aftermath* (New York: Farrar, Straus and Giroux, 2008). The other three stories have been constructed from information available in the literature and on the Internet.

22. Lev S. Vygotsky, *Mind and Society: The Development of Higher Mental Processes* (Cambridge, MA: Harvard University Press, 1978); David Wood, Jerome S. Bruner, and Gail Ross, "The Role of Tutoring in Problem Solving," *Journal of Child Psychology and Psychiatry* 17, no. 2 (1976): 89–100.
23. Prolepsis refers to foreshadowing the future in the present. The teacher acts as if learners have abilities that in fact they do not yet have. This (according to Vygotsky) is an essential condition for the development of those abilities; David Bakhurst, *Consciousness and Revolution in Soviet Philosophy: From the Bolsheviks to Evald Ilyenkov* (Cambridge: Cambridge University Press, 1991), 67.
24. Alexei Leontiev, quoted in Urie Bronfenbrenner, *The Ecology of Human Development* (Cambridge, MA: Harvard University Press, 1979), 40.
25. Deci and Flaste, *Why We Do What We Do.*
26. Vygotsky, *Mind and Society*; Denis Newman, Peg Griffin, and Michael Cole, *The Construction Zone: Working for Cognitive Change in School* (Cambridge: Cambridge University Press, 1989).
27. George C. Bunch, Aída Walqui, and P. David Pearson, "Complex Text and New Common Standards in the United States: Pedagogical Implications for English Learners," *TESOL Quarterly* 48, no. 3 (2014): 533–559.
28. Henry G. Widdowson, *Teaching Language as Communication* (Oxford, UK: Oxford University Press, 1978), 98.
29. Offered by Yasukata Yano, Michael H. Long, and Steven Ross, "The Effects of Simplified and Elaborated Texts on Foreign Language Reading Comprehension," *Language Learning* 44, no. 2 (1994): 189–219.
30. Substantive explorations of the nature of multimodal texts can be found in Jon Callow, *The Shape of Text to Come* (Sydney, AU: PETAA, 2013).

Chapter 3

1. A pseudonym is used.
2. Student names are pseudonyms.
3. This is the way in which dead languages (languages with no vitality, no native speakers) such as Latin are studied today.
4. The Lado/Fries method was developed at the University of Michigan in the mid-1960s; The distinction between *usage* and *use* was originally proposed by Henry G. Widdowson, *Teaching Language as Communication* (Oxford: Oxford University Press, 1978), 3. *Usage* is "that aspect of performance which makes evident the extent to which the language user demonstrates his knowledge of the linguistic rules" (phonological, lexical, and grammatical systems). *Use* is the aspect of performance which "makes evident the extent

to which the language user demonstrates his ability to use his knowledge of linguistic rules for effective communication."

5. In the 1950s and 1960s, second-language learners in the United States were not the focus of English as a second language efforts, but rather the "foreign" students came to the country to study at the university level. The study of English as a second language was typically carried out through courses of study in elite schools abroad with general educational interests, not necessarily within the US, nor for communicative purposes.

6. Noam Chomsky, *Syntactic Structures* (Oxford, UK: Mouton, 1957).

7. Stephen D. Krashen, *Second Language Acquisition and Second Language Learning* (Oxford, UK: Pergamon, 1981).

8. See, for example, Stephen D. Krashen, *Principles and Practice in Second Language Acquisition* (New York: Pergamon Press, 1982).

9. See, for example, Rebecca L. Oxford, "Use of Language Learning Strategies: A Synthesis of Studies with Implications for Strategy Training," *System* 17, no. 2 (1989): 235–247; Joan Rubin, "Study of Cognitive Processes in Second Language Learning," *Applied Linguistics* 11, no. 2 (1981): 117–131; Anita L. Wenden, "How to Be a Successful Language Learner: Insights and Prescriptions from L2 Learners," in *Learner Strategies in Language Learning*, ed. Anita L. Wenden and Joan Rubin (Englewood Cliffs, NJ: Prentice-Hall, 1987), 103–117.

10. Anna Uhl Chamot, *The CALLA Handbook: Implementing the Cognitive Academic Language Learning Approach*, 2nd ed. (White Plains, NY: Pearson Education/Longman, 2009).

11. Michael A. K. Halliday, *Learning How to Mean: Explorations in the Development of Language* (London: Edward Arnold, 1975); Dell H. Hymes, "On Communicative Competence," in *Sociolinguistics: Selected Readings*, ed. J. B. Pride and J. Holmes (Harmondsworth, UK: Penguin, 1972), 269–293.

12. Halliday, *Learning How to Mean*; J. L. Lemke, "Multimedia Semiotics: Genres for Science Education and Scientific Literacy," in *Developing Advanced Literacy in First and Second Languages: Meaning with Power*, ed. Mary J. Schleppegrell and M. Cecilia Colombi (Mahwah, NJ: Lawrence Erlbaum, 2002), 21–44; J. R. Martin and David Rose, *Working with Discourse: Meaning Beyond the Clause* (London: Continuum, 2007).

13. Mary J. Schleppegrell, *The Language of Schooling: A Functional Linguistics Perspective* (Mahwah, NJ: Erlbaum, 2004), ix.

14. Mary Schleppegrell, "Language in Academic Subject Areas and Classroom Instruction: What Is Academic Language and How Can We Teach It?" (invited paper, The National Research Council of the National Academy of Sciences, Menlo Park, CA, October 2009); See also Zhihui Fang, "Language Correlates of Disciplinary Literacy," *Topics in Language Disorders* 32, no. 1

(2012): 19–34; Schleppegrell, *The Language of Schooling*; Cynthia Shanahan, Timothy Shanahan, and Cynthia Misischia, "Analysis of Expert Readers in Three Disciplines: History, Mathematics, and Chemistry," *Journal of Literacy Research* 43, no. 4 (2011): 393–429.

15. Schleppegrell, "Language in Academic Subject Areas and Classroom Instruction," 7.

16. Ibid.

17. Pauline Jones and Honglin Chen argue that the New Australian Curriculum, ACARA, requires an awareness and knowledge about language that is not generalized in the country. "Teachers' Knowledge about Language: Issues of Pedagogy and Expertise," *Australian Journal of Language and Literacy* 31, no. 1 (2012): 149–170.

18. Lev S. Vygotsky, *Mind and Society: The Development of Higher Mental Processes* (Cambridge, MA: Harvard University Press, 1978).

19. Jean Lave and Etienne Wenger, *Situated Learning: Legitimate Peripheral Participation* (Cambridge: Cambridge University Press, 1991); Aída Walqui and Leo van Lier, *Scaffolding the Academic Success of Adolescent English Learners: A Pedagogy of Promise* (San Francisco, CA: WestEd, 2010); James P. Lantolf and Steven L. Thorne, *Sociocultural Theory and the Genesis of Second Language Development* (Oxford, UK: Oxford University Press, 2006).

20. These principles have been adapted from "Quality Teaching for English Learners Initiative," WestEd, www.wested.org/qtel.

21. The term "unnatural acts" has been used by Deborah Ball, Sam Wineburg, and others to refer to the development of teacher expertise that requires suspension of self, seeing from others' perspectives, simultaneously working with individuals and groups. See, for example, Deborah Loewenberg Ball and Francesca M. Forzani, "The Work of Teaching and the Challenge for Teacher Education," *Journal of Teacher Education* 60, no. 5 (2009): 497–511; Sam Wineburg, *Historical Thinking and Other Unnatural Acts: Charting the Future of Teaching the Past* (Philadelpia: Temple University Press, 2001). We are using it here to underscore the effort that it takes for teachers to challenge assumptions that have been unquestioned in the field for a long time.

22. Kenji Hakuta, "What Bilingual Education Has Taught the Experimental Psychologist: A Capsule Account in Honor of Joshua Fishman," in *Focus on Bilingual Education: Essays in Honor of Joshua Fishman*, ed. Ofelia García (Amsterdam: John Benjamins Publishing Company, 1991), 204; Guadalupe Valdés, "Bilingual Minorities and Language Issues in Writing: Toward Professionwide Responses to a New Challenge," *Written Communication* 9, no. 1 (1992): 85–136.

23. Center for Applied Language Studies (CASLS), *What Proficiency Level Do High School Students Achieve?* (Eugene, OR: CASLS, 2010); Diane

Larsen-Freeman and Diane Tedick, "Teaching World Languages," in *Handbook of Research on Teaching*, ed. Drew H. Gitomer and Courtney A. Bell (Washington, DC: American Educational Research Association, in preparation).

24. See, for example, Ofelia García, Susana Ibarra Johnson, and Kate Seltzer, *The Translanguaging Classroom* (Philadelphia: Caslon Press, forthcoming).

25. Jana Echevarria and Claude Goldenberg, "Teaching Secondary Language Minority Students" (Research Brief #4, Center for Research on Education, Diversity & Excellence, 1999), http://crede.berkeley.edu/pdf/rb04.pdf.

26. See, for example, Pam Grossman and Morva McDonald, "Back to the Future: Directions for Research in Teaching and Teacher Education," *American Educational Research Journal* 45, no. 1 (2008): 184–205.

27. Lee S. Shulman, "Those Who Understand: Knowledge Growth in Teaching," *Educational Researcher* 15, no. 2 (1986): 4–14.

28. Lee S. Shulman, "Knowledge and Teaching: Foundations of the New Reform," *Harvard Educational Review* 57, no. 1 (1987): 8.

29. Ibid.

30. See, for example, Aída Walqui, "The Development of Teachers' Understanding: Inservice Professional Development for Teachers of English Language Learners" (dissertation, Stanford, 1997); Aída Walqui, "The Development of Teacher Expertise to Work with Adolescent English Language Learners: A Model and a Few Priorities," in *Inclusive Pedagogy for English Language Learners: A Handbook of Research-Informed Practices*, ed. Lorrie Stoops Verplaetse and Naomi Migliacci (Mahwah, NJ: Lawrence Erlbaum, 2008), 103–125; Aída Walqui, "The Growth of Teacher Expertise for Teaching English Language Learners: A Socioculturally Based Professional Development Model," in *Teacher Preparation for Linguistically Diverse Classrooms: A Resource for Teacher Educators*, ed. Tamara Lucas (New York: Taylor & Francis, 2011), 15–52.

31. Kurt Lewin, *Field Theory in Social Science: Selected Theoretical Papers*, ed. Dorwin Cartwright (New York: Harper & Row, 1951), 169.

32. Leo van Lier, *The Ecology and Semiotics of Language Learning: A Sociocultural Perspective* (Dordrecht, NL: Kluwer Academic Press, 2004).

Chapter 4

1. Peter Elbow, "Writing First!" *Educational Leadership* 62, no. 2 (2004): 9–13.

2. James G. Greeno, Allan M. Collins, and Lauren B. Resnick, "Cognition and Learning," in *Handbook of Educational Psychology*, ed. David C. Berliner and Robert C. Calfee (New York: Macmillan, 1996), 15–46; John Seely Brown,

Allan M. Collins, and Paul Duguid, "Situated Cognition and the Culture of Learning," *Educational Researcher* 18, no. 1 (1989): 32–42.

3. For the earlier prevailing view, cf. John Dewey, *The Child and the Curriculum* (Chicago: The University of Chicago Press, 1902).

4. Mary James, "Assessment and Learning," in *Unlocking Assessment: Understanding for Reflection and Application*, ed. Sue Swaffield (New York: Routledge, 2008), 20–35.

5. Valentina Klenowski and Claire Wyatt-Smith, *Assessment for Education: Standards, Judgement and Moderation* (London: Sage, 2013).

6. Sue Swaffield, "Getting to the Heart of Authentic Assessment for Learning," *Assessment in Education: Principles, Policy and Practice* 18, no. 4 (2011): 433–449.

7. John A. Pitman, John E. O'Brien, and John E. McCollow, "High Quality Assessment: We Are What We Believe We Do" (paper presented at the International Association for Educational Assessment, Bled, Slovenia, May 1999).

8. Margaret Heritage, Aída Walqui, and Robert Linquanti, "Formative Assessment as Contingent Teaching and Learning: Perspectives on Assessment *As* and *For* Language Learning in the Content Area" (paper prepared for the Understanding Language Initiative, Stanford University, May 2013, ell.Stanford.edu/policy).

9. Caroline V. Gipps, *Beyond Testing: Towards a Theory of Educational Assessment* (London: The Falmer Press, 1994).

10. Swaffield, "Getting to the Heart."

11. Paul Black et al., *Assessment for Learning: Putting It into Practice* (New York: Open University Press, 2003); Dylan Wiliam, Clare Lee, Christine Harrison, and Paul Black, "Teachers Developing Assessment for Learning: Impact on Student Achievement," *Assessment in Education* 11, no. 1 (2004): 49–65; Mary James et al., *Improving Learning How to Learn: Classrooms, Schools and Networks* (London: Routledge, 2007); Christine Harrison and Sally Howard, *Inside the Primary Black Box: Assessment for Learning in Primary and Early Years Classrooms* (London: GL Assessment, 2009).

12. Paul J. Black and Dylan Wiliam, "Assessment and Classroom Learning," *Assessment in Education: Principles, Policy, and Practice* 5, no. 1 (1998): 7–73.

13. Ibid; Dylan Wiliam, "The Journey to Excellence," Education Scotland, http://www.journeytoexcellence.org.uk/videos/expertspeakers/selfandpeer-assessmentdylanwiliam.asp.

14. Elliot Eisner, *The Arts and the Creation of the Mind* (New Haven, CT: Yale University Press, 2002), 160.

15. Margaret Heritage, Sandy M. Chang, Barbara Jones, and Alison L. Bailey, "Investigating the Validity of Language Learning Progressions in Classroom Contexts" (paper presented at the annual meeting of the American Educational Research Association, Philadelphia, PA, April 7, 2014).

16. Margaret Heritage, *Formative Assessment in Practice* (Cambridge, MA: Harvard University Press, 2013).

17. Hugh Mehan, *Learning Lessons: Social Organization in the Classroom* (Cambridge, MA: Harvard University Press, 1979).

18. Frederick Erickson, "Some Thoughts on 'Proximal' Formative Assessment of Student Learning," *Yearbook of the National Society for the Study of Education* 106, no. 1 (2007): 186–216.

19. Tony Edwards, "Purposes and Characteristics of Whole-Class Dialogue," in *New Perspectives on Spoken English in the Classroom: Discussion Papers* (London: Qualifications and Curriculum Authority, 2003), 38–41.

20. Robin Alexander, "Learning to Talk, Talking to Learn," http://www.collaborativelearning.org/alexander.pdf.

21. National Research Council, *Knowing What Students Know: The Science of Design and Educational Assessment* (Washington, DC: National Academy Press, 2001); John Hattie, *Visible Learning for Teachers: Maximizing Impact on Learning* (New York: Routledge, 2009); John Hattie and Helen Timperley, "The Power of Feedback," *Review of Educational Research* 77, no. 1 (2007): 81–112.

22. Robert A. Baron, "Criticism (Informal Negative Feedback) as a Source of Perceived Unfairness in Organizations: Effects, Mechanisms, and Countermeasures," in *Justice in the Workplace: Approaching Fairness in Human Resource Management*, ed. Russell Cropanzano (Hillsdale, NJ: Lawrence Erlbaum, 1993), 155–170; Paul J. Black and Dylan Wiliam, "Inside the Black Box: Raising Standards Through Classroom Assessment," *Phi Delta Kappan* 80, no. 2 (1998): 139–148; Dylan Wiliam, "Keeping Learning on Track: Classroom Assessment and the Regulation of Learning," in *Second Handbook of Mathematics Teaching and Learning*, ed. Frank K. Lester Jr. (Greenwich, CT: Information Age Publishing, 2007), 1053–1098; Avraham N. Kluger and Angelo De Nisi, "The Effects of Feedback Interventions on Performance: A Historical Review, a Meta-Analysis, and a Preliminary Feedback Intervention Theory," *Psychological Bulletin* 119, no. 2 (1996): 254–284.

23. Hattie and Timperley, "The Power of Feedback."

24. Robin J. Alexander, *Towards Dialogic Teaching: Rethinking Classroom Talk*, 4th ed. (York, UK: Dialogos, 2008).

25. Philippe Perrenoud, "From Formative Evaluation to a Controlled Regulation of Learning Processes. Towards a Wider Conceptual Field," *Assessment in Education: Principles, Policy and Practice* 5, no. 1 (1998): 85–102.

26. Michael Absolum, *Clarity in the Classroom: Using Formative Assessment for Building Learning-Focused Relationships*, ed. James Gray and Meagan Mutchmor (Winnipeg, MB: Portage & Main Press, 2010).

27. Heidi Andrade and Anna Valtcheva, "Promoting Learning and Achievement Through Self-Assessment," *Theory Into Practice* 48, no. 1 (2009): 12–19.

28. Ernesto Panadero, Jesús Alonso-Tapia, and Eloísa Reche, "Rubrics vs. Self-Assessment Scripts Effect on Self-Regulation, Performance and Self-Efficacy in Pre-Service Teachers," *Studies in Educational Evaluation* 39, no. 3 (2013): 125–132.
29. Northwest Evaluation Association and Grunwald Associates LLC, "Make Assessment Matter: Students and Educators Want Tests That Support Learning," https://www.nwea.org/content/uploads/2014/04/MakeAssessment-Matter_5-2014.pdf.
30. Ibid.
31. Wiliam, "The Journey to Excellence."
32. Ibid.
33. Absolum, *Clarity in the Classroom.*

Chapter 5

1. *No Child Left Behind (NCLB) Act of 2001*, Public Law 107-110, *U.S. Statutes at Large* 115 (2002): 1961.
2. The definition of who is a potential ELL itself reflects a social construct that is likely the product of political negotiation.
3. Dafney Blanca Dabach and Rebecca M. Callahan, "Rights versus Reality: The Gap between Civil Rights and English Learners' High School Educational Opportunities," *Teachers College Record*, October 7, 2011, http://www.tcrecord.org/content.asp?contentid=16558; Kenji Hakuta, "Educating Language Minority Students and Affirming Their Equal Rights: Research and Practical Perspectives," *Educational Researcher* 40, no. 4 (2011): 163–174; Robert Linquanti and H. Gary Cook, *Toward a "Common Definition of English Learner": Guidance for States and State Assessment Consortia in Defining and Addressing Policy and Technical Issues and Options* (Washington, DC: Council of Chief State School Officers, 2013).
4. National Research Council, *Allocating Federal Funds for State Programs for English Language Learners* (Washington, DC: The National Academies Press, 2011).
5. The Race to the Top assessment consortia include the Smarter Balanced Assessment Consortium and the Partnership for Assessment of Readiness for College and Careers (PARCC). The two ELP assessment consortia funded by the federal Enhanced Assessment Grant program include the Assessment Services Supporting English Learners through Technology Systems (ASSETS) of the World-Class Instructional Design and Assessment (WIDA) Consortium, and the English-Language Proficiency Assessment for the 21st Century (ELPA 21) Consortium of the Council of Chief State School Officers

(CCSSO); Linquanti and Cook, *Toward a "Common Definition of English Learner."*

6. Kenji Hakuta and Alexandra Beatty, *Testing English-Language Learners in U.S. Schools* (Washington, DC: National Academy Press, 2000), 12–29; Jay P. Heubert and Robert M. Hauser, eds., *High Stakes: Testing for Tracking, Promotion, and Graduation* (Washington, DC: National Academy Press, 1999), 211–237.

7. David Francis, Tammy D. Tolar, and Karla K. Stuebing, "The Language-Achievement Connection for English Language Learners" (paper presented at the M3 Conference, Storrs, CT, May, 2011); U.S. Department of Education, Office of Planning, Evaluation and Policy Development, Policy and Program Studies Service, *National Evaluation of Title III Implementation Supplemental Report: Exploring Approaches to Setting English Language Proficiency Performance Criteria and Monitoring English Learner Progress*, by H. Gary Cook, Robert Linquanti, Marjorie Chinen, and Hyekyung Jung (Washington, DC, 2012)

8. According to this assessment's performance level descriptors, "intermediate" means students can understand some complex vocabulary and syntax, with occasional gaps in comprehension. They can follow some complex, multi-step oral directions and use a range of vocabulary and syntax appropriate to setting and purpose, with gaps in communication. They can tell a coherent story using phrases and incomplete sentences. They can use their knowledge of grammar and mechanics to identify appropriate words or phrases to complete a sentence. Their writing may contain errors in grammar, vocabulary, and/or syntax, while their compositions have a disorganized sequence of events, containing some details and repetitive transitional words.

9. "Early advanced" means students can understand extensive vocabulary and complex syntax, with occasional minor problems in comprehension. They can follow most complex, multistep oral directions and use fairly extensive vocabulary and fairly complex syntax appropriate to setting and purpose, with occasional minor errors. They can tell a coherent story using complete sentences with minor errors. They use their knowledge of grammar and mechanics to identify the appropriate word to complete a complex sentence. Their writing may contain minor errors in grammar and mechanics, while their compositions clearly communicate a series of events or ideas, have relevant details connected by accurate transitional words, and contain few errors in grammar and mechanics.

10. U.S. Department of Education, *National Evaluation of Title III Implementation Supplemental Report.*

11. See, for example, Rebecca M. Callahan, "Tracking and High School English Learners: Limiting Opportunity to Learn," *American Educational Research*

Journal 42, no. 2 (2005): 305–328; Ester J. de Jong, "After Exit: Academic Achievement Patterns of Former English Language Learners," *Education Policy Analysis Archives* 12, no. 50 (2004); Russell Rumberger and Patricia Gándara, "Seeking Equity in the Education of California's English Learners," *The Teachers College Record* 106, no. 10 (2004): 2032–2056.

12. National Research Council, *Allocating Federal Funds for State Programs for English Language Learners*; Mikyung Kim Wolf et al., *Issues in Assessing English Language Learners: English Language Proficiency Measures and Accommodation Uses*, CRESST Report 732 (Los Angeles: National Center for Research on Evaluation, Standards, and Student Testing, 2008); Working Group on ELL Policy, "Improving Educational Outcomes for English Language Learners: Recommendations for the Reauthorization of the Elementary and Secondary Education Act, Questions and Answers," http://ellpolicy. org/wp-content/uploads/QA.pdf.

13. Megan Hopkins et al., "Fully Accounting for English Learner Performance: A Key Issue in ESEA Reauthorization," *Educational Researcher* 42, no. 2 (2013): 101–108; Robert Linquanti and Kenji Hakuta, *How Next-Generation Standards and Assessments Can Foster Success for California's English Learners*, Policy Brief 12-1 (Stanford, CA: Policy Analysis for California Education, July 2012); William M. Saunders and David J. Marcelletti, "The Gap That Can't Go Away: The Catch-22 of Reclassification in Monitoring the Progress of English Learners," *Educational Evaluation and Policy Analysis* 35, no. 2 (2013): 139–156.

14. Hopkins et al., "Fully Accounting for English Learner Performance"; Saunders and Marcelletti, "The Gap That Can't Go Away."

15. Saunders and Marcelletti, "The Gap That Can't Go Away."

16. Marianne Perie, Scott Marion, and Brian Gong, "Moving Toward a Comprehensive Assessment System: A Framework for Considering Interim Assessments," *Educational Measurement: Issues and Practice* 28, no. 3 (2009): 5–13.

17. Council of Chief State School Officers, *Interim Assessment Practices and Avenues for State Involvement* (Washington, DC: CCSSO, 2008).

18. Lorrie A. Shepard, "Commentary: Evaluating the Validity of Formative and Interim Assessment," *Educational Measurement: Issues and Practice* 28, no. 3 (2009): 32–37; Perie et al., "Moving Toward a Comprehensive Assessment System."

19. Council of Chief State School Officers, *Distinguishing Formative Assessment from Other Educational Assessment Labels* (Washington, DC: CCSSO, 2012), 12.

20. Adapted from California Department of Education, *English Language Arts/ English Language Development Instructional Framework*, http://www.cde.ca .gov/ci/rl/cf/documents/chapter8sbeadopted.pdf, 21–22.

21. Ibid., 23.
22. Robert Linquanti, "Strengthening Assessment for English Learner Success: How Can the Promise of the Common Core State Standards and Innovative Assessment Systems Be Realized?" in *The Road Ahead for State Assessments*, ed. David Plank and Jill Norton (Palo Alto, CA: Policy Analysis for California Education and Rennie Center for Education Research & Policy, 2011), 13–25; Lorrie A. Shepard, "Formative Assessment: Caveat Emptor" (presentation at the ETS Invitational Conference 2005, The Future of Assessment: Shaping Teaching and Learning, New York, NY, October 10–11, 2005); Shepard, "Linking Formative Assessment to Scaffolding," *Educational Leadership* 63, no. 3 (2005): 66–70; Shepard, "Commentary"; Lauress L. Wise, "Picking Up the Pieces: Aggregating Results from Through-Course Assessments" (paper commissioned by the Center for K–12 Assessment & Performance Management at ETS, Princeton, NJ, 2011).
23. Richard P. Durán, "Assessing English-Language Learners' Achievement," *Review of Research in Education* 32, no. 1 (2008): 292–327; Rebecca Kopriva, *Improving Testing for English Language Learners* (New York: Taylor & Francis, 2008); National Research Council, *How People Learn: Brain, Mind, Experience, and School* (Washington, DC: National Academy Press, 2000).
24. Jamal Abedi and Robert Linquanti, "Issues and Opportunities in Improving the Quality of Large Scale Assessment Systems for English Language Learners," in *Understanding Language: Commissioned Papers on Language and Literacy Issues in the Common Core State Standards and Next Generation Science Standards*, ed. Kenji Hakuta and María Santos (Palo Alto, CA: Stanford University, 2012), 75–85.
25. Hopkins et al., "Fully Accounting for English Learner Performance"; Working Group on ELL Policy, "Improving Educational Outcomes for English Language Learners."
26. See, for example, Texas's ELP and academic progress expectations and monitoring system at http://www.tea.state.tx.us/student.assessment/ell/. See also Hopkins et al., "Fully Accounting for English Learner Performance"; Robert Linquanti, "Fostering Success for English Learners in Turnaround Schools: What State Education Agencies Need to Know and Be Able to Do," in *The State Role in School Turnaround: Emerging Best Practices*, ed. Lauren Morando Rhim and Sam Redding (Charlotte, NC: Information Age Publishing, 2014), 207–222; Working Group on ELL Policy, "Improving Educational Outcomes for English Language Learners."
27. H. Gary Cook and Rita MacDonald, "Tool to Evaluate Language Complexity of Test Items" (presented at the 2012 Center for Research on the Educational Achievement and Teaching of English Language Learners (CREATE) Conference, Orlando, FL, October 2012); H. Gary Cook and Rita MacDonald,

"Using the Language Complexity Tool to Guide Item Writing" (webinar presented to the Smarter Balanced Assessment Consortium, October 24, 2012). Note that the tool developed by Cook and MacDonald is different in design and purpose than text complexity rating tools such as the Lexile system.

28. Construct-irrelevant language interference refers to unnecessarily complex and confusing language forms and structures that do not target or contribute to the construct that is being measured.

29. Abedi and Linquanti, "Issues and Opportunities in Improving the Quality of Large Scale Assessment Systems"; Linquanti, "Strengthening Assessment for English Learner Success."

30. Smarter Balanced Assessment Consortium, "Usability, Accessibility, and Accommodations Guidelines," http://www.smarterbalanced.org/wordpress/wp-content/uploads/2014/03/SmarterBalanced_Guidelines_091113.pdf.

31. Jamal Abedi, "Language Issues in the Design of Accessible Items," in *Handbook of Accessible Achievement Tests for All Students: Bridging the Gaps Between Research, Practice, and Policy*, ed. Stephen N. Elliott et al. (New York: Springer, 2011), 217–230; Jamal Abedi, "The Use of Computer Technology in Designing Appropriate Test Accommodations for English Language Learners," *Applied Measurement in Education* 27, no. 4 (2014): 261–272.

32. Linquanti and Cook, *Toward a "Common Definition of English Learner."*

33. Robert Linquanti and Alison L. Bailey, "Reprising the Home Language Survey: Summary of a National Working Session on Policies, Practices, and Tools for Identifying Potential English Learners" (Washington, DC: Council of Chief State School Officers, 2014).

34. H. Gary Cook and Rita MacDonald, "Reference Performance Level Descriptors: Outcome of a National Working Session on Defining an 'English Proficient' Performance Standard" (Washington, DC: Council of Chief State School Officers, 2014); H. Gary Cook and Robert Linquanti, "Strengthening Policies and Practices for the Initial Classification of English Learners: Insights from a National Working Session" (Washington, DC: Council of Chief State School Officers, 2014).

35. U.S. Department of Education, *National Evaluation of Title III Implementation Supplemental Report.*

36. Linquanti and Cook, *Toward a "Common Definition of English Learner."*

37. See, for example, Alison L. Bailey, Kimberly Reynolds Kelly, Sandy Chang, and Margaret Heritage, "Empirical Study of Elementary Student Explanations: Generating Dynamic Language Learning Progressions" (paper presented at the annual meeting of the American Educational Research Association, Philadelphia, PA, April 2014); Cynthia Greenleaf and Thomas Hanson, "READi: Reading, Evidence, and Argumentation in Disciplinary Instruction," http://www.wested.org/research_study/readi-reading-evidence-and-argumentation-in-disciplinary-instruction/; Margaret Heritage, "Learning

Progressions: Supporting Instruction and Formative Assessment" (paper prepared for the Formative Assessment for Teachers and Students (FAST) State Collaborative on Assessment and Student Standards (SCASS) of the Council of Chief State School Officers, Washington, DC, 2008); Margaret Heritage, Sandy Chang, and Barbara Jones, "Investigating the Validity of Language Learning Progressions in Classroom Contexts" (paper presented at the annual meeting of the American Educational Research Association, Philadelphia, PA, April 2014).

38. Linda Darling-Hammond and Frank Adamson, *Beyond the Bubble Test: How Performance Assessments Improve Teaching and Learning* (San Francisco: Jossey-Bass, 2014); National Education Association, "Preparing 21st Century Students for a Global Society: An Educator's Guide to the 'Four Cs,'" http://www.nea.org/assets/docs/A-Guide-to-Four-Cs.pdf; North Central Regional Educational Laboratory (NCREL) and the Metiri Group, "enGauge 21st Century Skills: Literacy in the Digital Age," http://pict.sdsu.edu/engauge21st.pdf; Partnership for 21st Century Skills, "Learning for the 21st Century: A Report and Mile Guide for 21st Century Skills," http://www.p21.org/storage/documents/P21_Report.pdf.

Chapter 6

1. See California Department of Education, "A Deeper Dive into the California ELD Standards, Unit 6." California Common Core State Standards: Professional Learning Modules, http://www.myboe.org/portal/default/Content/Viewer/Content?action=2&scId=509621.
2. Title I is a section of the Elementary and Secondary Education Act (ESEA) of 1965 that seeks to ensure all children have access to a high-quality education. Title I outlines a number of methods to ameliorate differences in achievement between groups of students, including children from low-income communities and underachieving populations.
3. The overarching purpose of Title III, also part of ESEA, is to ensure that English language learners reach English proficiency and have access to a high-quality education where they are expected to meet the same standards of achievement as other students. Title III also allocates funding for instructional programs for ELLs.
4. Patricia Gándara and Megan Hopkins, eds., *Forbidden Language: English Learners and Restrictive Language Policies* (New York: Teachers College Press, 2010).
5. Richard Elmore, *School Reform from the Inside Out* (Cambridge, MA: Harvard Education Press, 2004).
6. Richard Elmore, *I Used to Think . . . and Now I Think . . . : Twenty Leading*

Educators Reflect on the Work of School Reform (Cambridge, MA: Harvard Education Press, 2011).

7. Jal Mehta, *The Allure of Order: High Hopes, Dashed Expectations, and the Troubled Quest to Remake American Schooling* (New York: Oxford University Press, 2013), 250.

8. Elmore, *School Reform from the Inside Out*; Mehta, *The Allure of Order*.

9. National Research Council, *How People Learn: Brain, Mind, Experience, and School* (Washington, DC: National Academy Press, 2000); National Research Council, *Knowing What Students Know: The Science and Design of Educational Assessment* (Washington, DC: National Academy Press, 2001); National Research Council, *Education for Life and Work: Developing Transferable Knowledge and Skills in the 21st Century* (Washington, DC: National Academy Press, 2013).

10. Mehta, *The Allure of Order*, 269–294.

11. Ibid., 274.

12. Andy Hargreaves and Michael Fullan, *Professional Capital: Transforming Teaching in Every School* (New York: Teachers College Press, 2012), 88–102.

13. Anthony Bryk et al., *Organizing Schools for Improvement: Lessons from Chicago* (Chicago: University of Chicago Press, 2009).

14. Brentt Brown and Merrill Vargo, *Designing, Leading, and Managing the Transition to the Common Core: A Strategy Guidebook for Leaders* (Palo Alto, CA: Policy Analysis for California Education, 2014).

15. Eric Nadelstern (CEO of the New York City Empowerment Zone), in discussion with Aída Walqui, June 2004.

16. Mike W. Kirst, *The Common Core Meets State Policy: This Changes Almost Everything* (Palo Alto, CA: Policy Analysis for California Education, 2013).

17. Milbrey McLaughlin, Laura Glaab, and Isabel Hilliger Carrasco, *Implementing Common Core State Standards in California: A Report from the Field* (Palo Alto, CA: Policy Analysis for California Education, 2014).

18. Brentt Brown and Merrill Vargo, *Getting to the Core: How Early Implementers Are Approaching the Common Core in California* (Palo Alto, CA: Policy Analysis for California Education, 2014); Michael Fullan, *Stratosphere: Integrating Technology, Pedagogy, and Change Knowledge* (Toronto, ON: Pearson, 2012); McLaughlin et al., *Implementing Common Core State Standards in California*.

19. Robert Linquanti, "Supporting Formative Assessment for Deeper Learning: A Primer for Policymakers" (paper prepared for the Formative Assessment for Students and Teachers (FAST) State Collaborative for Assessment and Student Standards (SCASS) of the Council of Chief State School Officers, Washington, DC, 2014).

20. Linda Darling-Hammond et al., *Professional Learning in the Learning Profession* (Palo Alto, CA: National Staff Development Council, 2009); Linquanti,

"Supporting Formative Assessment for Deeper Learning"; María Santos, Linda Darling-Hammond, and Tina Cheuk, "Teacher Development to Support English Language Learners in the Context of the Common Core," in *Understanding Language: Commissioned Papers on Language and Literacy Issues in the Common Core State Standards and Next Generation Science Standards*, ed. Kenji Hakuta and María Santos (Palo Alto, CA: Stanford University, 2012), 104–114.

21. Tamara Holmund Nelson et al., "Leading Deep Conversations in Collaborative Inquiry Groups," *The Clearinghouse: A Journal of Educational Strategies, Issues and Ideas* 83, no. 5 (2010): 175–179.

22. Ibid., 178–179. An abridged version of the article, with graphical representations of collegial dialogue process versus congenial conversations, may be found at: http://www.myboe.org/portal/default/Resources/Viewer/Res ourceViewer?action=2&resid=510291. These and other questions related to examining assessment practices and reflection on group process are found in the unabridged version.

23. For an example of how formative assessment practices are being incorporated into preservice teachers' clinical curriculum and teaching experiences, see Brent Duckor, "Formative Assessment in Seven Good Moves," *Educational Leadership* 71, no. 6 (2014): 28–32.

24. George C. Bunch, "Pedagogical Language Knowledge: Preparing Mainstream Teachers for English Learners in the New Standards Era," *Review of Research in Education* 37, (2013): 298–341; Santos et al., "Teacher Development."

25. Santos et al., "Teacher Development," 109.

26. Martin Orland and Jan Anderson, *Assessment for Learning: What Policymakers Should Know About Formative Assessment* (San Francisco: WestEd, 2013).

27. For an example of how one state is revising its ELL accountability provisions in light of new standards and assessments, see the Texas Education Agency model available at http://www.tea.state.tx.us/student.assessment/ ell/, and specifically, http://www.tea.state.tx.us/WorkArea/linkit.aspx?Link Identifier=id&ItemID=25769810177&libID=25769810190; see also Working Group on ELL Policy, "Improving Educational Outcomes for English Language Learners: Recommendations for the Reauthorization of the Elementary and Secondary Education Act, Questions and Answers," http://ellpolicy .org/wp-content/uploads/QA.pdf.

28. For a review of the problematic evidence base for value-added measures and other teacher evaluation approaches using test score growth, see Linda Darling-Hammond, *Getting Teacher Evaluation Right: What Really Matters for Effectiveness and Improvement* (New York: Teachers College Press, 2013).

29. Measures of Effective Teaching (MET) Project, *Asking Students about Teaching: Student Perception Surveys and Their Implementation*. Policy and

Practice Brief (Seattle, WA: Bill & Melinda Gates Foundation, 2012); Measures of Effective Teaching (MET) Project, *Ensuring Fair and Reliable Measures of Effective Teaching: Culminating Findings from the MET Project's Three-Year Study.* Policy and Practice Brief (Seattle, WA: Bill & Melinda Gates Foundation, 2013).

30. As with the use of any observation protocol, observers (whether peers or administrators) of formative assessment practices need sufficient training and certification prior to making consequential observations, and periodic calibration opportunities to ensure consistency and accuracy over time.

31. The MET Project report (2012) illustrates a local model that integrates teacher formative evaluation, instructional videotaping, student survey feedback, and teacher in-class coaching. Also, examples of age-specific student survey questions that are coherent with and provide feedback to teachers on the formative assessment process can be found in Rick Stiggins and W. James Popham, "Assessing Students' Affect Related to Assessment for Learning: An Introduction for Teachers" (paper released through the Formative Assessment for Teachers and Students (FAST) State Collaborative on Assessment and Student Standards (SCASS) of the Council of Chief State School Officers (CCSSO), Washington, DC, 2007).

32. Such reciprocal accountability acknowledges that neither teachers nor students can perform as expected without developing the capacity to do so, and neither can develop that capacity without appropriate support. Properly designed, funded, and integrated policies and systems of professional learning and formative evaluation are key to this reciprocity; Elmore, *School Reform from the Inside Out.*

33. MET Project, *Asking Students*, 4.

34. Gary L. Anderson and Kathryn Herr, "Scaling Up 'Evidence-Based' Practices for Teachers Is a Profitable but Discredited Paradigm," *Educational Researcher* 40, no. 6 (2011): 287–289.

35. Nevada Department of Education, "Nevada Educator Performance Framework: Teacher and Administrator Standards," http://www.doe.nv.gov/Boards_Commissions_Councils/Teachers_and_Leaders_Council/2013_Agenda_and_Minutes/Resources_Library/Nevada_Ed_Performance_Framework/2013_08_NEPF_TEACHER_AND_ADMIN_STANDARDS/; "Nevada Educator Performance Framework (NEPF) Statewide Evaluation System, Teacher and Administrator Protocols/Tools: For Training and Validation Purposes," http://www.doe.nv.gov/Boards_Commissions_Councils/Teachers_and_Leaders_Council/2014/September/NEPF_Tools__Protocols-Sept_2014_(1)/.

Acknowledgments

◆

Each of us owes a debt of gratitude to several people.

Margaret's appreciative thanks go to all the teachers who are represented throughout the book, and particularly to Gabriela Cardenas and Olivia Lozano, who have helped her learn about pedagogy and formative assessment with English language learners from the work they do every day with their students. She is deeply indebted to Alison Bailey, a friend and colleague for many years, who has taught her so much about language. She has a special word of thanks for John Heritage for his invaluable support, encouragement, and understanding.

This book is dedicated to Leo van Lier. His influence on Aída's work on language and pedagogy is ever present. His vast knowledge and insight, his unique way of integrating and relating diverse fields, his modesty, his wonderful teaching, his commitment, all continue to be a source of inspiration for her. She extends her appreciative thanks to the many teachers she has worked with, especially colleagues at the International Newcomer Academy in Fort Worth, Texas. Her conversations with members of the Understanding Language initiative—in particular, Guadalupe Valdés, George Bunch, and Amanda Kibler—have been enormously beneficial. Her special thanks go to Kenji Hakuta, who has provided intellectual and personal support for the last three decades. She is indebted to the Quality Teaching for English Learners team at WestEd, whose daily work models the dialogic and intimate nature of conceptual, analytical, and linguistic development.

Robert has benefited from collaborating with, and gratefully acknowledges his fellow members of, the Understanding Language initiative and the Working Group on English Language Learner Policy. In particular, he thanks Gary Cook for his extraordinary collegiality and Kenji Hakuta for his perennial friendship and metaphors. He also thanks Pam Spycher and his coauthors for helping him see how, at the end of the day, it is and must be about the learner. He especially thanks Geni Solla, whose love, support, and companionship matter most.

At Harvard Education Press, we thank Caroline Chauncey for her prompt reviews of each chapter and for her tremendously helpful feedback. The book is truly a better one for all the time and thought she committed to the review process. We are especially grateful to Sandy Chang, Julie Park Haubner, Maritza Lozano, and Nicole Mancevice for their invaluable assistance in the preparation of the manuscript. Finally, we offer our special thanks to Kenji Hakuta. His invitation to develop a paper for the Understanding Language initiative and our resulting collaboration led to this book. We are delighted he has written the foreword.

About the Authors

———————— ◆ ————————

Margaret Heritage is senior scientist at WestEd and assistant director at the National Center for Research on Evaluation, Standards, and Student Testing at the University of California, Los Angeles. For many years her work has focused on formative assessment and on how teachers can implement effective formative assessment in their classrooms. She has made numerous presentations all over the United States, as well as in Europe, Asia, and Australia, and has published extensively on the topic. Her last book, *Formative Assessment in Practice: A Process of Inquiry and Action*, was also published by Harvard Education Press.

Aída Walqui directs the Teacher Professional Development Program at WestEd. She specializes in the professional growth required by teachers to work with second-language learners deeply and generatively. Her work has focused on defining, designing, and supporting quality education in multilingual, intercultural contexts in the United States, Europe, Asia, and Latin America. She has published extensively on issues related to teacher professional development and the development of deep literacies with English language learners.

Robert Linquanti is project director and senior researcher at WestEd. His work helps educators and policy makers at local, state, and national levels to strengthen assessment, evaluation, and accountability policies, practices, and systems for English language learners. He has published and presented widely on evaluating education policies, establishing comprehensive assessment systems, and improving accountability and equity for ELLs. He serves on several state and national advisory bodies related to these topics.

Index

♦